A Theology for Married Couples

A Theology for Married Couples:
The Shadow of the Eternal Marriage

Copyright © 2025 by Ryul J. Kwon

Published by Overflowing Joy
  #402, Yelim Bldg, 9, Supyo-ro 2-gil, Jung-gu,
  Seoul, 04554, Republic of Korea

All rights reserved.
This book was published out of Overflowing Joy (샘솟는기쁨)
an exclusive contract with the copyright holder. Unauthorized
reproduction and reproduction are prohibited because the
work is protected in Korea under the copyright law.

Publisher: Young Ran Kang
Editor: Gwan Yong Park, Ji Yeon Kwon
Design: TRINITY
Marketing & Management: Jin Ho Lee

E-mail: atfeel@hanmail.net
Facebook: https://www.facebook.com/publisherjoy

The first edition was published on May 12, 2025.
Originally this book was published in Korean in 2025.

ISBN 979-11-92794-58-7(03190)

A THEOLOGY FOR MARRIED COUPLES

The Shadow of the Eternal Marriage

Ryul J. Kwon

샘솟는
기쁨

Let Us Put Our Hope
In the Lord Alone

Sharing my life with a man is like entering a strange world. I entered that world thanks to the Holy Spirit who put love in my heart when I was dating before marriage, but as it turned out, the marriage was never easy. I came to my senses one day after the birth of my first child. I thought, "Why am I here? How did I end up being a pastor's wife? All sorts of complicated thoughts went through my head, but it was too late.

For more than half of my 20-year marriage, my husband and I have had a hard time quarreling, and I've often said to him that our marriage is like a lottery. It means that nothing is a match. When we were dating, I was blinded by love and thought we were a good match, but the hard realities of marriage made me realize that we were not compatible. As a pastor's wife, I had to do almost all of the childcare by myself, which made my unspeakable struggles even worse.

But now I am so happy. I don't just say that "in faith" because I'm a pastor's wife, but I'm genuinely happy and thankful every day. Of course, there are times when I feel sad, but it's only because we misunderstood each other for a while. The blunt husband who didn't know the woman very well has now become a little more domestic than I thought he would be, and has made his wife feel better. It seems that my husband changes as I live patiently.

My husband has always been the same. He lives his life immersed in what he believes is right before God. He's a very unique person who doesn't enjoy life outside of the Bible and missions, but maybe that's why I love him so much. I used to struggle with his consistency. Twelve years ago, he was a workaholic in ministry and neglected his family, but now, amazingly, he is just as busy in ministry as he was then and still knows how to love his wife. I think it's because he was reborn from a workaholic to a person with a mission, as he says in this book. Normally, I am very spontaneous and impulsive, but now I feel more stable because of my husband's character, and I am very happy.

I used to find it very strange to see my husband talking about the kingdom of God as if he were from another world. But now, we are living our daily lives together, dreaming of the kingdom of God. Five years ago, the whole family was preparing to go to the

Philippines as missionaries without any doubts, but the coronavirus pandemic canceled the plan. Since then, we have been living like a missionary family in Korea. Even though our life is not as stable as that of church workers, I am very happy with my current life with my husband. Although I am a pastor's wife, sometimes I feel that I am living like a layperson, which is not so bad.

When my husband wrote *A Theology for Married Couples*, he said that he needed the wife's foreword. He said that readers of *A Theology of Dating* are curious to know how much his wife agrees with the content of the book. I can confidently say that I was moved to marry my husband because of the peculiar letter he wrote to me when we were dating, and I still wholeheartedly agree with everything in *A Theology for Married Couples*. I hope that every married couple in the world will read this book and restore their relationship as beautifully as we did. Especially wives, let us no longer put our hope in our husbands, but only in the Lord, and with that determination, you will find your husband as loving as I did.

Mi Ae Son, the Author's Wife

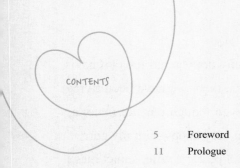

CONTENTS

A Workaholic Husband | "You know I Still Love You, Right?" | Loving God & Loving Spouse | The Touchstone to Diagnose Spiritual State | Apply with the Fear of God | They Have Become, But Need to Become | A Triangle with God as the Apex

■ Questions for Sharing and Application

Does a Couple's Love Never Change? | What Is the Will to Love Between a Couple? | Because of the Covenant, Not the Love of the Couple | Does Marriage Change a Man? | Marriage Changes a Woman Too!

■ Questions for Sharing and Application

Three Elements of Covenant Marriage | When a Man Won't Leave His Parents | Filial Piety Requires a Good Marriage | When a Man Does Not Unite with His Wife | When a Couple Doesn't Become One Flesh | Church Women Tamed by Asceticism | God-Given, Beautiful Sexual Desire | Sexual Desire and Lust Are Different! | Sexual Desire and Covenant | Lust Is Idolatry | Experience Holy Affection

■ Questions for Sharing and Application

The Sequel to *A Theology of Dating*, Finally Released!

It has been years since *A Theology of Dating* was published. I am very happy that it is still being read and loved by readers. I have heard that readers often ask when the sequel will come out. Some of them are already married and raising children, and now they want to read a book about marriage from the perspective of *A Theology of Dating*. So I feel a little late, but I am finally releasing its sequel.

I would like to explain the nature of *A Theology for Married Couples*. This book focuses, as the title suggests, on married couples. While there is some theological analysis of marriage in general, the focus is on how married couples actually interact and respond to each other. This distinguishes it from John Piper's *This Momentary Marriage*. My book, *A Theology for Married Couples* is a biblical, doctrinal, and somewhat counseling approach to the various situations and problems that married couples face.

This book is much more practical and down-to-earth than *A Theology of Dating*. While it focuses more on theological interpretations and doctrines, *A Theology for Married Couples* focuses more on real-life examples. I have counseled many couples and have summarized their experiences in the simplest possible language. For the record, all the characters in this book are pseudonyms to protect them, and the content of the counseling has been simplified as much as possible, excluding unnecessary parts. In no case, however, is the author's depiction of fictionalized situations.

In fact, I'm hardly qualified to write this book. Although I had a peculiar dating before marriage, I had to face during the marriage many of the problems that stemmed from my dysfunctional childhood. Watching my parents' failed marriage, I vowed never to emulate it. But I failed too. I was often horrified to see my father's disposition bursting out of me toward my wife and children. Fortunately, the dysfunctional parts of my life have been offset by the love of God that I have experienced. Now, after 20 years of marriage, I am a different man thanks to God's love and my wife's constant caring.

So half of *A Theology for Married Couples* is actually my wife's contribution. When I was finalizing the manuscript, I realized that I needed her foreword more than anyone else. She has written a heartfelt and very sincere foreword. I want it to be a testimonial that proves to the readers that the content of this book is true.

Each chapter ends with questions for sharing and application. These are questions that would be useful in a book club for married couples. In addition to these questions, readers are encouraged to create their own questions for discussion. I would love nothing more than for couples to read this book together and enjoy the spiritual benefits of sharing with each other. And unless otherwise noted, this book uses the NKJV Bible.

Finally, I would like to thank some people who made this book possible. I am especially grateful to the CEO of Overflowing Joy (샘솟는기쁨) for publishing it as a beautiful book in English. I would also like to express my sincere gratitude to Go Sun Eum (Pastor Baek's wife) for reading and commenting on the manuscript I translated from the Korean version (『부부 신학』). And I dedicate this book to my wife, Mi Ae Son, and my three sons, who have been actively supporting my writing ministry more than anyone else.

Ryul J. Kwon

March 26, 2025

22 Then the rib which the LORD God had taken from man He made into a woman, and He brought her to the man.

23 And Adam said:

"This *is* now bone of my bones
And flesh of my flesh;
She shall be called Woman,
Because she was taken out of Man."

24 Therefore a man shall leave his father and mother and be joined to his wife, and they shall become one flesh.

_Genesis 2:22-24, NKJV

CHAPTER 1

Becoming a True Couple

♡ A Workaholic Husband

It was the last day of May, 2013. In the morning, my wife spoke to me with an urgent look on her face.

"Honey, the hospital called and said I have stomach cancer."

"What?"

I jumped up, stunned, even though I was sound asleep. I tried to calm her down and reassure her that we should go to another hospital and have another test. But the results at the other hospital were the same.

The news that my wife had been diagnosed with stomach cancer was like slamming on the brakes while driving. I was half forced to put down the ministries I had been immersed in, and I realized how neglectful I had been of my wife. As a staff member of a campus ministry organization, I didn't see my family for half the year. I would spend time with students and come home late at night to find my family asleep, and in the morning I would wake up first thing and rush to campus. Even during vacations, I was often away for various retreats and meetings, and when I had some free time, I would lie down like a corpse all day because I was tired.

All this was to me a "great" mission for the kingdom of God. I thought my wife would be happy to support my ministry and strive to do the housework taking care of the children.

But I was completely wrong! As it turned out, she was forced to support my ministry because she was a pastor's wife, and she could barely keep up with the housework and childcare with little help from me. Even in this situation, I was obsessed with a noble sense of mission and put more energy into the ministry. In addition, the lack of communication hurt her feelings. I couldn't remember the last time we had a heart-to-heart conversation. When she told me she had stomach cancer, I focused on her words.

I thought I was on a mission, but I was actually a workaholic. If you have a strong perfectionism, achievement-oriented personality, and a strong tendency to get lost in your work, especially to escape from your spouse and family, you're practically a workaholic. That's exactly what I was.

A sense of mission and workaholism are like fraternal twins. They both come from the same passion in the same person, just in different directions. A burning sense of mission directs that energy to the God who gave it to us, while workaholism directs it to the person who is drowning in it. On the surface, both produce remarkable results, so it's not easy to tell the difference without looking at the inner motivations. This is especially true of the person doing the work.

A burning sense of mission increases our love for God because it directs our energy toward Him. As our love for God grows, our love for our spouse grows proportionately, because loving God and loving our spouse can never be separated. (More on this in a moment.) So the more we are consumed by a burning sense of mission, the more we are consumed by a passionate love for our spouse. You must realize that one of the purposes of marriage is to live as a couple with a mission for the kingdom of God.

Workaholism, on the other hand, directs energy to the workaholic so that his soul suffers from an inner emptiness. In other words, his inner being is filled with self-love. But there is a space within us that can only be filled with God's love. Because the workaholic tries to fill that space with self-love, he feels like he's filled with something, but because it's not God's love, he ends up empty inside. This leaves no room in our hearts to love our spouse, because our love for our spouse is based on God's love. Loving God and loving our spouse are always connected, so if one is wrong, the other will always be wrong.

Twelve years ago, I was exactly what I was: a workaholic. I was directing my energies inward, filling myself with self-love instead of God's love, fooling myself into thinking it was a burning sense of mission. My workaholic self-love filled my soul with an inner emptiness that left no room in my heart to love my spouse.

The life event that made me self-aware was my wife's diagnosis with stomach cancer. Fortunately, I found a great doctor, her surgery was successful, and she is now in remission and living a healthy life. It is now one of my life's goals to make my wife happy, the one who made her workaholic husband sober.

♡ "You know I Still Love You, Right?"

Looking back now, I realize that 12 years ago, when I was in a workaholic state, my relationship with my wife was really bad, but I didn't think so at that time. I secretly thought that a good relationship with my wife would prevent me from living as a person with a mission. This is a typical Confucian mindset: that husband and wife should be different from each other, that there is a strict division between them rather than closeness, and that the wife in particular should understand and follow what her husband does.

This mentality almost inevitably drives people of my temperament toward workaholism. In this case, the relationship with the spouse begins to become estranged, and it is difficult to expect an intimate couple relationship. The wife becomes a mere adjunct to her husband's work, who shouldn't interfere.

At the time, I tried to ignore my wife's difficulties. I thought it was the role of a pastor's wife to joyfully endure such hard work for the kingdom of God and the church. I thought she was struggling because she didn't have enough faith. It was a breakdown in communication!

No wonder our relationship was suffering. We weren't able to share any kind of lover's whispers other than casual conversation. I was overwhelmed by my ministry schedule and reacted irritably to my wife, and she reacted irritably to me because she was tired of parenting. Even in this state, I prayed to God as if there was nothing wrong with my faith.

God, You know I still love you, right?

I comforted myself for a while, convinced that God was pleased with me. I firmly believed that even if my wife didn't know my heart, God knew my heart and was with me, comforting me, because I thought I was faithfully fulfilling the mission God had given me.

One day I was praying in my room, still in a bad relationship with my wife.

God, I work harder than anyone and I am faithful to the mission You have given me. Even though my wife doesn't understand me now, I firmly believe that one day You will change her heart. You know that no matter how bad my relationship with my wife is, I still love You.

But at that moment, I began to feel a "voice" within me.

Jonathan, will you stop this abominable prayer at once?

I was embarrassed and pondered what this meant. I wondered why my prayer was abominable. Was it abominable if I hadn't been more sincere? But the answer lay elsewhere.

Loving God & Loving Spouse

Loving God and loving your spouse are inseparable. In a sense, they are the same thing. This is covered in *A Theology of Dating*,[1] but I'll go into more detail. Let's look at Ephesians 5:31-32 (NKJV), which is often used as the main text for weddings.

> [31] *"For this reason a man shall leave his father and mother and be joined to his wife, and the two shall become one flesh."* [32] This is a great mystery, but I speak concerning Christ and the church.

As you may recognize, verse 31 is Paul's quotation of Genesis 2:24, and verse 32 is a commentary on that verse (Gen. 2:24). In other words, God created the institution of marriage, the union of husband and wife (v. 31), which means "the great mystery," and

---

★

1)   Ryul J. Kwon, *A Theology of Dating* (Seoul: Overflowing Joy, 2022), 38-40.

the reason marriage is a great mystery is because it ultimately speaks of Christ and the church (v. 32). In particular, a couple in marriage should show us what Christ is like and what His beloved church should be like.

This means that marriage and faith are inseparable. A life of faith is a way of life that shows how we, as the beloved of Christ, serve Him in our daily lives. As we see in the verse above, this life of faith is always intertwined with the great mystery of husband and wife's marriage. To put it simply, you can tell their life of faith by their marriage.

In a more personalized way, it means that I cannot separate my love for my spouse from my love for God. Jesus also spoke of this principle in a general sense. In Matthew 22, when a lawyer tried to test Jesus by asking, "Teacher, which is the great commandment in the law?" (v. 36), Jesus boiled it down to two commandments.

> 37 Jesus said to him, " *'You shall love the LORD your God with all your heart, with all your soul, and with all your mind.'* 38 This is *the* first and great commandment. 39 And *the* second *is* like it: *'You shall love your neighbor as yourself.'* 40 On these two commandments hang all the Law and the Prophets." (Matt. 22:37-40)

As you can see, Jesus says that loving the LORD our God is "*the* first and great commandment." But then He adds, "*the* second *is* like it." The second commandment is to love our neighbor as ourselves, as it immediately follows. We should focus on His Word that the second commandment is like the first.

Of course, this does not mean that the two commandments are exactly the same in every respect. How can they be identical in every aspect and content when the object of love is God and the object of love is man? To translate the Greek text vividly, it means, "And the second commandment is no different from the first" (δευτέρα δὲ ὁμοία αὐτῇ). In simpler terms, loving God and loving our neighbor are not exactly the same in every respect, but loving our neighbor is no different from loving God. This also means that you can't love one or the other. Loving your spouse is included in the second commandment to love your neighbor. So loving your spouse is no different than loving God!

If we look more closely at the statement, "the second commandment is no different from the first," we find a principle of love. The statement that loving God and loving our neighbor are not identical in all respects tells us where love comes from. It means that loving our neighbor comes from loving God. (Of course, non-Christians say they love their neighbor in a general sense.) In other words, loving our neighbor is no different from loving God, but loving our neighbor comes from loving God.

Let's apply this principle back to marriage. If I love my

spouse, that means I now love God. What if we reverse this? If I do not love my spouse, it means that I do not love God "rightly."

Earlier, I described an experience in which God rebuked me for my prayers as an abomination. God was not pleased with my prayers 12 years ago when I was in a broken relationship with my wife and prayed fervently, "God, You know I still love you, right?" Why? Because my love for God was distorted at that moment.

I thought it was possible to love God independently of my spouse, but God declares that it is impossible! I thought that God would comfort my heart and accept "my heart that still loves God," even if my relationship with my wife went wrong, but He said that it is impossible. This is because if I don't love my wife rightly, it means that I don't love God rightly.

This becomes even clearer when we consider the passage from Ephesians mentioned earlier. The apostle Paul said that the mystical union of Christ and the church should be revealed through the relationship between husband and wife. So what happens if there is a serious crisis between a husband and wife? In such a state, they can never reveal who Christ is and what the church should be. On the contrary, it would blaspheme Christ and dishonor the church. In short, problems in your marriage will lead to problems in your faith. We must remember that the two are always intertwined.

That's why it's impossible to love God apart from your spouse!

When I was in college, I saw the irony of a famous preacher. He preached to young people with great eloquence and knowledge, but he seemed to take some pride in telling them about his own divorce: He had decided to divorce his wife because he felt that her spiritual state during their marriage was not up to his standards. Even though his sermon was gracious, that one word completely shut me down. To my ears, it sounded like the relationship between Christ and the church could be severed in that way. Christ never abandons His bride, the church, even when she is not whole! In any case, the preacher was in direct violation of Ephesians, which says that the relationship between God and the preacher should be demonstrated in his marriage.

The Touchstone to Diagnose Spiritual State

So what is the touchstone by which we can diagnose our spiritual state right now? It is the way we are currently treating our spouse. Consider His providence that the relationship between Christ and the church, that is, between God and us, must be demonstrated through the relationship between husband and wife.

This is a great mystery, but I speak concerning Christ and the church. (Eph. 5:32)

Are you treating your wife roughly? You must know that you have such an attitude toward God who created your wife! Are you ignoring your husband in a subtle way? You must know that you have such an attitude toward God who created your husband!

Does this application seem like overkill? Not at all. Jesus applies what we do to our brothers and sisters, we do to you, not only in marriage, but in all relationships. In Matthew 25:31, Jesus says that He will return to this world in glory with all His angels. Then He will gather all people before Him, and He will separate the righteous from the wicked, who will go to eternal life and everlasting punishment. To the righteous who have cared for their brothers and sisters and satisfied their hunger and thirst, Jesus said:

'Assuredly, I say to you, inasmuch as you did *it* to one of the least of these My brethren, you did *it* to Me.' (Matt. 25:40)

In other words, what they did to satisfy their brother's hunger and thirst was what they did to Jesus. As you can see from the above passage, Jesus identifies Himself with "one of the least of these." Why would He do that? Because one of the least of these is part of His body. The phrase "these My brethren" refers to all believers who have been bonded by the blood of Christ.[2] That is to say, the church, the body of Christ. That's why Jesus considers even "one of the least of these My brethren" to be Himself.

So what if we reverse the above verse? Whatever you did not do to one of the least of these, you did not do to Jesus. In fact, that's what Jesus said.

'Assuredly, I say to you, inasmuch as you did not do *it* to one of the least of these, you did not do *it* to Me.' (Matt. 25:45)

Jesus said to the wicked, "for I was hungry and you gave Me no food; I was thirsty and you gave Me no drink; I was a stranger and you did not take Me in, naked and you did not clothe Me, sick and in prison and you did not visit Me.' " (25:42-43). The implication is that when "one of the least" of the body of Christ is in such a condition, even though He never hungers or thirsts, He immediately considers Himself to be in such a condition.

If so, we need to ponder. It is the relationship between husband and wife that reveals the relationship between Christ and the church in the deepest and most intimate way. If Jesus applied that principle (identifying with Himself) to all His brothers and sisters in Christ, shouldn't it apply even more so to the marriage relationship?

Since husband and wife are technically part of the body of

★

2)　양용의, 『마태복음 어떻게 읽을 것인가(개정판)』 (서울: 한국성서유니온선교회, 2018), 498.

Christ, Jesus' phrase "one of the least of these" naturally applies to married couples. Now, husbands and wives who believe they are part of the body of Christ should ask themselves. Can you sense Jesus' identification of Himself with your spouse? Would you recognize that what you have done to your spouse is what you have done to Jesus? And would you recognize that what you have not done to your spouse is what you have not done to Jesus?

That's a terrible thing to say, especially when I apply it to myself 12 years ago.

> Jonathan, you were not with Me when I was hard and lonely; you did not help Me when I was raising My children, not knowing that I had stomach cancer; you did not help Me when I was enduring and shedding tears out of caring for you; you kept turning away My tears.

Once again, I offer a counsel to husbands and wives who believe in Jesus. If you want to diagnose your spiritual state, look at how you are treating your spouse. Your attitude toward your spouse is your attitude toward God. You may not realize it. Seriously, just ask your spouse and you'll see. If the answer is that he/she is happy to live with you in Christ, then your spiritual state is one that is filled with the love of God. This is because your love for God is transmitted to your spouse as a feeling of happiness.

However, if your spouse hesitates to answer or changes the subject, you should seriously consider your own spiritual state. To put it bluntly, because you don't love God very much, you don't love your spouse, the body of Christ, very much. We should always seek the heart of Christ, who identifies Himself with your spouse.

Apply with the Fear of God

There is a warning to applying the principle of identifying your spouse with Christ Himself. It does not mean that you should conform unconditionally to your spouse, regardless of his/her condition. As noted in *A Theology of Dating*, the Christian marriage is a love triangle with God as the apex.[3] From the very first wedding, God joined Adam and Eve together as husband and wife and set them up in such a relationship — that is, to exist as spouses to one another in the presence of God and in constant awareness of God.

As we apply the principle of identifying our spouse with Christ Himself to our marriage, then, we should seek to foster a God-fearing attitude in each other. Paul exhorted us to submit "to one another in the fear of God" (Eph. 5:21). (Coincidentally, this ex-

★
3) Ryul J. Kwon, *A Theology of Dating*, 110.

hortation is immediately followed by an exhortation to both wives and husbands.) Even as husbands and wives submit to one another, they should do so in a state of reverence for Christ who is God.

What would happen if a husband does not fear God, but his wife unconditionally conforms and submits to him? It is very likely that she will be used by her husband's impure intentions. Conversely, what would happen if a wife does not fear God, but her husband unconditionally submits to her? She may be happy for the time being, but he is likely to be used by her intentions.

God wants husbands and wives to be constantly attuned to each other in a state of reverence for Him. This is important to remember when applying the principle of identifying your spouse with Christ Himself. Because the husband is the body of Christ and the wife is the body of Christ, both the husband and the wife should be looking to Christ. See the image of Christ in each other and endeavor to tolerate and love each other with the same eyes with which He sees you. Only then will you be able to identify your spouse with Christ Himself and receive from him/her an accurate diagnosis of your spiritual state.

 **They Have Become, But Need to Become**

There's no relationship that's as weird and strange as a married couple. They love each other so much that they get married, but at some point, they start to fall apart, fighting like they've never seen each other before, and even splitting up. Why is this? Because they have become a married couple, but they didn't become an actual couple.

That is to say, they've entered into the "legal relationship" of being a married couple, but they haven't lived the "actual relationship" of being a couple. It is not just the moment of becoming a married couple that matters, but the process of becoming a couple that matters even more. This is like saying that a wedding and a marriage are different. A wedding is a "one-day event" that makes you a couple, but a marriage is a "long period of life" that you actually live as a couple.

These same qualities apply to our life of faith. Our faith is our spiritual marriage to Jesus, our Bridegroom. The Bible frequently compares the relationship between Jesus as God and us as the church to that of a husband and wife.[4]

Spiritual marriage is the process by which a sinner lives as one body with the holy Jesus. In order for this to be possible, the sinner must first experience saving grace, which is the forgiveness of sins and acceptance by God as righteous. This is called "justification," which is a theological term for our legal status: a legal

---

★

4) Isa. 54:5; Jer. 3:14; Hos. 2:16; Matt. 9:15; John 3:29; 2 Cor. 11:2.

declaration that Jesus and we are one body, and the first moment when He, the Bridegroom, accepts us as His bride.

But it doesn't end there. The process of actually living as one body with the Bridegroom begins immediately. This process of becoming holy like Him is called sanctification. Justification is a momentary, legal declaration, but sanctification is an ongoing, actual change.

Similarly, there is a moment when a couple is legally declared to be spouses, and immediately after that the process of becoming an actual couple begins. It's important for brides and grooms, especially those who are about to marry or have just begun their marriage, to be able to distinguish between the two. The bride and groom are not the finished spouses they see on their wedding day; they are the ones who are still in the process of becoming actual spouses to each other.

The same is true of our faith. We are not instantly made holy like the angels in heaven the moment we believe in Jesus and are born again. In other words, the church, with Christ as her Bridegroom, is not transformed into perfection at the moment she becomes His bride. She has a glorious status immediately upon conversion, but she must continue to be sanctified in order to be perfected to be worthy of that status.

It seems natural that these theological principles would apply to the marriage relationship. It is God's providence to reveal the relationship between Christ and the church through the relationship of husband and wife (Eph. 5:31-32). That is, the long process of becoming an actual couple, as the husband and wife who have entered into the legal relationship, should show how the church, the legal bride of Christ, is actually becoming the holy church.

The bride and groom must learn to live as a couple for the rest of their lives, not just the moment they become husband and wife. In other words, they have become a married couple, but they need to become an actual couple. This is always intertwined with the principles of our faith. Therefore, the key to a good marriage is a good life of faith, and vice versa. (In fact, we should emphasize this more.) The key to a good life of faith is a good marriage. Why? Because, as mentioned earlier, loving God and loving spouse are inseparable.

A Triangle with God as the Apex

The Christian marriage is a triangle with God as the apex. This also applies to relationships before marriage. Many church members struggle or fail in their marriages because they only think of the horizontal relationship between husband and wife.

But a married couple should always think about their vertical relationship with God. Our very existence was created that way.

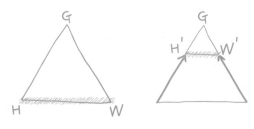

The Triangle of Love

The Triangle of Love[5] from *A Theology of Dating* is here again.

As you may have guessed, the three vertices represent God, Husband, and Wife, respectively. Husband and Wife are horizontally united with each other, but as the figure shows, they are also vertically united with God respectively. (Of course, it's not vertical, it's 60° in the figure.) With God as the apex, the husband and wife are never in a one-to-one relationship, but always in a triangle.

The Triangle of Love illustrates the changing distance between a married couple. We can see that in order for a husband and wife to become more intimate, they need to move closer to God, who is at the apex. In the figure on the right, as Husband and Wife each move closer to God, the line segment H'W' becomes shorter than the line segment HW, meaning that the couple becomes closer. Conversely, if the Husband and Wife each move further away from God, the distance between them increases.

Why is this? Because when a husband seeks spiritual intimacy with God, he uses that energy to love his wife more. Likewise, when a wife enjoys spiritual intimacy with God, she uses that energy to love her husband more.

However, there is a strong tendency to perceive it as the opposite during the dating before marriage and the early stages of the honeymoon. This is because the state of sexual arousal that comes with the secretion of love hormones can be so powerful that it overtakes spiritual intimacy with God, or "spiritual arousal." This is why they feel so strongly drawn to each other, away from God and toward each other. In reality, they are not. But such a state doesn't last as long as they think. The love hormones diminish over time, and eventually they realize that they are unable to love each other passionately with the energy inherent in them.

This ultimately leads to a longing for God, the source of love. They earnestly desire the love of God to be poured out in their hearts through the Holy Spirit (Rom. 5:5). If this desire or longing is not present at all, there is something seriously wrong with his/her faith. We must be empowered to love our spouse with the love that the Holy Spirit pours out. At first we thought that the love of the couple sustained the relationship, but it turns out that the love of God sustains the relationship.

1. Describe a time when you were so engrossed in your work that you were tempted to avoid your spouse and children.

2. Feel free to share the difference between a sense of mission and workaholism.

3. How do you currently treat your spouse and how much do you love him/her? Do you recognize that this mindset and attitude is your current level of love for God?

4. Are you satisfied with the legal fact that you have become a married couple? Or are you taking concrete steps to become an actual couple? Be honest about what you are doing to live as a biblical couple.

CHAPTER 2

A Couple's Love Can Change

♡ Does a Couple's Love Never Change?

In my counseling practice, I often hear wives say, "He's the same as he was in our dating before marriage!" And some husbands assure that their wives love them just as much now as they did when dating. While it would be great if these statements were sincere, many times they are not. In fact, it's very likely that one party is "killing" themselves by putting up with the other to avoid conflict.

We need to free ourselves from the idealized hope that the love of a married couple will never change. Rather, we should recognize that love is in fact variable. So what is it about a couple's love that causes it to change over time?

A Theology of Dating explains in detail that the forms of love are will and emotion.[6] In particular, the emotion of love is directly related to the secretion of love hormones. So when the secretion of hormones ceases, the emotional state toward the spouse will necessarily change. This is not to say that love itself changes, but that the emotional state of the two components that make up love is different than before. This is where couples often misunderstand and grumble.

"My husband has changed since we got married!"

★

6)   Ryul J. Kwon, *A Theology of Dating*, 53-69.

"He didn't do it when we were dating, but I don't know why he does it now."

"My wife is nagging me more and more."

"I guess dating and marriage are different after all."

If you deeply analyze these comments, you'll find that they're annoying because the emotion of love is not what it used to be. When the love hormones were high, anything they said or did seemed adorable, but now that the love hormones are depleted, the rose-colored glasses come off.

At this point, we don't need to think that love itself has changed. Although the emotion of love is very important, it's more of a chemical reaction of hormonal secretions and can change depending on your body and health. It can even decrease and then increase again.

However, will is more essential to love than emotion. The will to love is essential to a marriage, as it sustains the wavering emotions of love as hormones are secreted. A professor of psychiatry once said, "Even without hormones, love will not disappear as long as there is a human will."[7] This means that even if your emotional state changes with hormonal secretions, your will to love may not change.

★

7)   송웅달, 『900일간의 폭풍 사랑』 (서울: 김영사, 2007), 68. I translated the Korean sentence into English.

But the will to love is strongly influenced by our emotional state. Even if you have a strong will to love your spouse, if you don't have the emotion of love, your will to love will gradually lose its power. The emotion of love is a result of hormones that your body produces on its own, but it is also strongly triggered by receiving deep attention and care from your spouse. If these emotions or feelings of love do not continue to arise, can the will to love be fully rooted in you? In other words, can you maintain your will to love your husband if your emotions are constantly being hurt by his ruthless behavior? Or can you maintain your will to love your wife if your emotions are constantly being hurt by her constant nagging?

If it continues without improvement, the couple's love will eventually change, because both components (will and emotion) of love will change. In fact, it's a common phenomenon that all couples experience when their emotional state changes with hormonal fluctuations. To put it bluntly, you don't make love as often as you used to. And even if you do make love more often, it's hard to feel the same thrill in the bedroom as you did when you were newlyweds. There's nothing wrong with this phenomenon.

The problem is that they stop caring deeply for their spouse because the emotions of love cool down according to the decrease of the love hormones. People who fantasize about "pure" love are more prone to this problem. They say that anything that is artificial and not accompanied by emotions of love is not love. While their logic may seem plausible at first glance, it's really just an excuse to say that their body is no longer producing love hormones, and that it's harder for them to care for their spouse.

This is something husbands need to pay attention to, especially since wives consider attention and care to be a great love language. While men often feel their emotions of love soar when their sexual instincts are stimulated, women feel more powerful emotions of love when sexual stimulation is accompanied by deep attention and care.

In any case, you need to get rid of the illusion that a couple's love can continue unchanged. Although the will to love is much more unchangeable than the emotions of love, it's important to remember that even the will to love, which is strongly influenced by emotional states, is sometimes difficult to sustain. To summarize, you shouldn't assume that you've changed just because your emotions of love are less than they used to be. You should also remember that your love is faltering if you use this as an excuse to withhold attention and care from your spouse, thereby hurting his/her emotions and thus breaking the will to love.

What Is the Will to Love Between a Couple?

The emotions of love that arise between lovers or couples

don't need to be explained. They are a natural response that flows from the bodies of a man and a woman who have fallen in love. However, the will to love requires a more detailed explanation. In *A Theology of Dating*, I only briefly mentioned the will to love.[8] I did not emphasize the will to love in the premarital period because the emotions of love account for much more during the dating stage.

Now, in keeping with the title of this book, I will focus on the theology for married couples. The will to love between a Christian couple refers to the couple's inner desire to dream of the kingdom of God and to reveal to the world the relationship between Christ and the church, based on the covenant of marriage. Let me explain what I mean.

First, the will to love is based on the covenant of marriage. That is to say, the will to love is rooted in the marriage covenant. The Christian marriage is a covenant between a bride and groom made before God. It is a divine promise that can never be broken, except in exceptional cases such as adultery. (Of course, even if a spouse has committed adultery, he/she should do everything possible to restore the relationship.) On the covenant is based the will of the groom to love the bride and of the bride to love the groom. The entire wedding is a covenant ceremony, but the "vows" and

★

8) Ryul J. Kwon, *A Theology of Dating*, 80.

the "pronouncement" are at the heart of a covenant marriage.[9] Since a covenant made before God cannot be broken, the will to love rooted in that covenant must remain virtually unchanged.

Next, the will to love between a couple leads them to dream of the kingdom of God. The first human couple was in the Garden of Eden, the prototype of the kingdom of God. And in this world, which is now "Paradise Lost," every couple dreams of the perfect kingdom of God that will be consummated in the future. Married couples dream together of the day when not only the place[10] where our souls enter after death, but also the place where we are currently stepping on will become the glorious God's kingdom with the Lord's return. If a Christian couple does not think about this at all, then their marriage has some other purpose.

Finally, the will to love in a couple is an inner desire to reveal to the world the relationship between Christ and the church. This has already been mentioned several times. As the Lord revealed to Paul, the institution of marriage is a great mystery because it ultimately reveals the mystical union of Christ and the church (Eph. 5:31-32). The will of a couple to love each other is a holy commitment to bear witness with their whole being to what Christ is

---

★

9)   In this book, I use the term *covenant marriage* to emphasize the marriage of covenantal nature and *marriage covenant* to emphasize the covenantal nature of marriage.

10) In theological terms, it is called the *intermediate state* and is described in the Bible as "Paradise" or the "third heaven" (Luke 23:43; 2 Cor. 12:2,4).

and what the church should be through their marriage.

The will to love that exists between a husband and wife is not merely a casual determination to love each other. Their will to love each other is rooted in the holy covenant, and unless that covenant is broken, their will to love must remain unchanged. This will is manifested in their desire for the kingdom of God and the church. A Christian couple should have this will to love for each other.

♡ Because of the Covenant,
Not the Love of the Couple

Earlier, we argued that a couple's love can change. We saw that the will to love, as well as the emotion of love, can be affected by the emotional state and can waver and change. Therefore, it is not a couple's love that sustains a marriage. Rather, it is the "covenant" of marriage that holds the couple's love together. Even when a couple's love falters, it is the covenant that keeps their marriage together.

Think about it. If a marriage is said to last because the husband loves his wife, does it immediately cease to exist if the husband no longer loves his wife? Likewise, if a marriage is sustained because the wife loves her husband, does it immediately cease to exist if she no longer loves him?

Absolutely not! A couple stays married because of the covenant they made before God, even if they no longer love each other. To put it simply, because they promised God that they would stay together, they honor that promise, even if they no longer love each other. That's why the marriage covenant is what sustains the couple's relationship and holds them together so that their love can be restored.

The same principle applies to our faith. Our faith is not maintained because we love God. That might be possible if our love for God never changed, but as we all confess, our love for Him often changes. So it is impossible to think that our faith depends on this shallow love. Rather, our faith is sustained because of the covenant that He, the Bridegroom, has made with us; that is, our love for Him does not sustain our faith, but His covenant[11] with us sustains our faith.

God never breaks His covenant. "My covenant I will not break, Nor alter the word that has gone out of My lips." (Ps. 89:34). Based on this covenant, a husband and a wife are each in a spiritual marriage with God (a vertical relationship). The covenant that each of them has with God can be described as the *vertical*

★

11) For more information about God's covenant with us, see the answer to Q. 31 in the Westminster Larger Catechism and the answer to Q. 20 in the Shorter Catechism.

covenant. The vertical covenant is interlocked with the marriage covenant between the couple (horizontal relationship). The covenant between the couple is called the *horizontal covenant.* So the horizontal covenant, which is the marriage covenant, is based on the vertical covenant that can never be broken. It sounds complicated, but the principle of this covenant is the same as *The Triangle of Love* mentioned earlier. Let's rephrase it as *The Triangle of Covenant.*

The Triangle of Covenant

Now we have discovered why the marriage covenant cannot be broken: as shown in the diagram, the horizontal covenant (i.e., the marriage covenant) between the couple is interlocked with the vertical covenant that can never be broken. It is this structure that allows a marriage to survive, even if the couple's love falters. From the unbreakable vertical covenant comes the strength to support the horizontal covenant, which in turn sustains the couple's love.

But what if a husband no longer loves his wife, and what if a wife is no longer able to love her husband? There are times in a marriage when a couple faces such a crisis. What should a couple who believes in God do in such a situation?

They must first realize why they are the way they are. If a husband does not love his wife, it is almost inevitably because he does not love God rightly. Recall the principle that loving God and loving one's spouse are inseparable. And if a wife does not love her husband, it is almost certainly because she does not love God rightly.

Marital crises occur because couples do not love God rightly, except in special cases. When a husband and a wife each love God passionately, they are willing to tolerate and love their spouse because of that love. When we are "spiritualized" with God's love, we are able to look at our spouse with love, just as we would when dating before marriage. There comes a point in a marriage when the emotions of love caused by the secretion of love hormones dissipate, so it is impossible to continue to love your spouse with the emotions of love that you generate within yourself.

Therefore, couples in crisis should pray fervently that they will love God fervently. They must remember Paul's admonition that God's love is poured out in our hearts through the Holy Spirit (Rom. 5:5). Couples in crisis should desperately cling to God's

Holy Spirit to awaken them to be faithful again to their marriage covenant. Recognize that even the most intense love can change over time, and pray together that God, who is faithful to His covenant, will preserve the couple's love.

♥ Does Marriage Change a Man?

There's a saying that most married women will tell you. They say that their husbands change after marriage. I completely agree, but I would like to defend man's character for a moment.

When a man really loves a woman, he enters a powerful state of sexual arousal, which means that his love hormones spike rapidly, usually to a much greater degree than women's. (Of course, there are some men and women who don't.) When he's full of love hormones, he starts to say and do things like never before. And they come naturally to him, not by force or effort. He doesn't feel tired or exhausted, even if he's on a crazy date schedule. He looks at her through the rose-colored glasses!

But it doesn't last as long as you might think. Studies have shown that married couples stay romantically in love for an average of two years.[12] In any case, once the honeymoon period passes

★
12) 게리 채프먼, 『5가지 사랑의 언어』 장동숙 외 옮김 (서울: 생명의말씀사, 2010), 37.

and the secretion of love hormones decreases dramatically, men's loving behavior disappears. At this point, the men don't really change, they just go back to being themselves. More precisely, they return to the state they were in before they started dating. They almost return to their normal selves before they met their wives.

This may sound sad to women, but from that point on, men's will to love is much stronger than their emotions of love. In other words, they become more inclined to treat their wives as a duty of love. Not just a duty, of course, but a "duty of love." Nevertheless, wives expect the same "emotions" of love from their husbands as before. So husbands try their best to live up to that expectation. However, when they find themselves unable to return to their previous state of love hormones, they blame themselves and despair.

Wives should not assume that their husbands' love has cooled or changed. Rather think that a different aspect of love has begun to emerge. The same goes for the husbands themselves. There's no need to despair or beat yourself up over it. Once again, it's not just the hormonal emotions of love that make up a couple's love. It's important to remember that while there is rarely a strong state of sexual arousal outside of marital sex, a couple's willingness to be faithful to their marriage covenant and their care and concern for each other is a much larger part of their love. If husbands remain unchanged in these areas, wives need not doubt their husbands' love.

♀Marriage Changes a Woman Too!

Wives say that husbands change when they get married, but wives change too. This is because wives are also affected by the secretion of love hormones. Neither men nor women can remain at the peak of their love hormones. It's biologically impossible. Even if you've been married for a long time, you don't always feel the same excitement and heart palpitations as you did when you were dating or newlyweds. If your heart is still racing like it was when you were in dating, it's most likely an arrhythmia and you should see a doctor.

We need to recognize the differences in temperament between men and women. In general, men are much more goal-oriented and achievement-oriented than women. Some social psychologists interpret this in terms of social evolution,[13] but it's better to understand it as a difference in male and female sexual psychology. When men are sexually stimulated, they want to reach the final stage (climax) of ejaculation without stopping. Once they reach their goal, they relax and quickly return to their original state. This sexual psychology and pattern reflects the goal-oriented temperament of men.

★

13) The idea is that since ancient times, men have been primarily engaged in risk-taking, competition, and fighting, which has led to a goal-oriented and achievement-oriented temperament. 로이 F. 바우마이스터, 『소모되는 남자』, 서은국 외 옮김 (서울: 시그마북스, 2015), 386-387.

On the other hand, when women are sexually stimulated, they don't have a single stage of ejaculation like men do. Rather, they experience multiple climaxes (orgasms), and the sexual afterglow lasts much longer than men, even after sex. This sexual psychology and reaction reflects the process-oriented temperament of women.

Now let's summarize the expected reactions of married men and women. Men feel like they've "accomplished" everything because they've reached the "goal" of marriage. So they're relaxed and quite laid back, unlike before. Women, on the other hand, imagine in their minds the "process" that "begins"now that they're married, and they still want to enjoy the romantic afterglow with their husband, just as they did when they were dating. In short, men think of marriage as an "end" (fulfillment, relief) and women think of marriage as a "beginning" (process, anticipation).

This is why wives say that their husbands have changed. When they see their husbands return to their original, relaxed selves, relieved to have achieved the biggest goal of their lives, that is, marriage, wives realize that the romantic days they expected upon marriage were an illusion. So, in their eyes, their husbands have definitely changed. But the husbands who hear the wives' nagging from this point on also think that their wives have changed, because they are clearly different from their pre-marital relationships.

1. Do you think a married couple's love changes? Or do you think it may never change? If then, in what ways do you think so?

2. Share honestly what you think your spouse has changed compared to before you got married.

3. Explain again what this chapter means by "the will to love that exists between a married couple."

4. What do you think makes a couple's relationship work and keeps it that way?

Leave, Unite, and Become One

🛏 Three Elements of Covenant Marriage

Genesis 2 introduces humanity's first wedding. God causes Adam to fall into a deep sleep, takes one of his ribs, creates a woman, and brings her to Adam (vv. 21-22). The sight overwhelms Adam with joy, and he sings the first human "wedding song."

> And Adam said:
> "This *is* now bone of my bones
> And flesh of my flesh;
> She shall be called Woman,
> Because she was taken out of Man." (Gen. 2:23)

It's a beautiful song sung by the bridegroom Adam to his bride. "This *is* now bone of my bones and flesh of my flesh" is a covenantal statement of Adam's unwavering commitment to his bride, whether she is strong or weak.[14] Here we see that the first human marriage is already a covenant. Adam says that he will call her woman because her body came from him and will never be separated from him (the man). Then the next verse begins.

★

14) Victor P. Hamilton, *The Book of Genesis, Chapters 1-17*, NICOT (Grand Rapids, MI: William B. Eerdmans, 1990), 180.

Therefore a man shall leave his father and mother and be joined to his wife, and they shall become one flesh. (Gen 2:24)

"Therefore" here means "from the fact that Adam and Eve were created in such a way and came into the world and entered into such a relationship."[15] In other words, Adam and Eve were created by God Himself and set up in an inseparable relationship with each other. This is what Genesis 2:24 says.

This verse, the first statement about marriage, lists the three elements of covenant marriage. The phrase "three elements of covenant marriage" means that Christian marriage is a holy covenant before God, and there are three elements that must be present for the covenant of marriage to be established. That is, they are what make a marriage acceptable to God. Let's take a look at them one by one.

First, marriage is when a man leaves his parents. This in itself is radical, given the climate of patriarchal society in the ancient Near East at the time Genesis was written. Furthermore, the Hebrew verb for "to leave," *azab* (עָזַב), is often used in the Old Testament to describe the Israelites' rejection of their covenant relationship with the LORD God.[16] When a man leaves his parents,

★

15) 황영철, 『이 비밀이 크도다』 (의정부: 드림북, 2017), 32. I translated the Korean sentence into English.

16) Jer. 1:16; 2:13,17,19; 5:7; 16:11; 17:13, etc. Victor P. Hamilton, *The Book of Genesis, Chapters 1-17*, 181.

then, it means that he ceases to be covenantally loyal to them. Of course, it doesn't mean that he should cut off his relationship with his parents. It means that he is now in control of his life and independent (or self-reliant) of his parents in all aspects.

Second, marriage is the joining (union) of a man to his wife. The Hebrew verb for "to join" is *dabaq* (דבק), which means to solder with two pieces of metal to make them stick together.[17] This means to keep the covenant relationship intact,[18] as opposed to "to leave." In this case, it means that a man ceases to fulfill his covenantal loyalty to his parents and now fulfills it to his wife. The covenantal separation of "to leave" is followed by the covenantal joining of "to unite." The covenantal union of husband and wife includes both sexual and emotional intimacy.

Third, marriage is the equal becoming one flesh of a man and his wife. This means more than just sexual intercourse. It means that the couple shares everything in each other. If you look closely at the verse above (Gen. 2:24), the subject is "a man" until the stages of leaving and union. That is, a man shall leave his parents and be united (or joined) to his wife. But now the subject is "they." In other words, the man and his wife are on an equal footing and "they shall become one flesh." The idea of equal footing here is

★

17) Ray Ortlund, *Marriage and the Mystery of the Gospel*, ed. Dane C. Ortlund and Miles Van Pelt, Short Studies in Biblical Theology (Wheaton, IL: Crossway, 2016), 30.

18) Deut. 4:4; 10:20; 11:22; 13:4, etc.

due to Adam's confession in verse 23, "She shall be called Woman, Because she was taken out of Man." When Adam, a man, gave his wife the name woman, he was "not affirming his sovereignty, but recognizing that she was a being of equal status with him."[19]

To summarize, the three elements of covenant marriage are "to leave, to unite, and to become one flesh." All three are connected, meaning that "to leave" necessarily results in "to unite," and "to unite" necessarily results in "to become one flesh." God recognizes the Christian marriage as having these three elements. Since God has established these three as the principles of marriage, not only for Christians but for all mankind, if anyone does not follow these principles, there will be problems in marriage, both great and small.

When a Man Won't Leave His Parents

It happened many years ago when I was serving as an associate pastor in a church. I was on call in the church office one Monday when a sister visited, looking very pale. She introduced herself as Jane. (As I said in the prologue, all the names in this book are pseudonyms.) Even though I didn't know her, I knew intuitively

---

★

19) 송병현, 『엑스포지멘터리 창세기』 (서울: 국제제자훈련원, 2010), 120. I translated the Korean sentence into English.

that she was in deep trouble.

She was a young housewife in her late 20s, still in a dysfunctional marriage. She had recently stamped the divorce papers and was contemplating divorce. Her husband's immature behavior and her mother-in-law's domineering behavior made it impossible for her to live a normal life. Whenever she raised her voice, her husband would scream and act strangely, even calling his mother for help. Whenever there is a conflict between the couple, instead of talking to his wife, he always reports the situation to his mother for advice.

Moreover, her mother-in-law's violent intervention further alienated the couple. Normally, when a married son reacts like that, the parents would be the ones who would have to discipline their son. But her mother-in-law one-sidedly covered up her son and tried to force a divorce. Shockingly, she was a senior deaconess! Jane suddenly said.

> Pastor, what will happen to my children in the future? I am most worried about the hurt they will suffer because of the sin I have committed. What will the future hold for my little children?

As a pastor, I sincerely empathized with her, comforted her, and gave her some realistic advice. I revealed that I was also a child of a divorced family and told her how I overcame my emotional wounds. In fact, my father, who is now deceased, tried to resolve his marital conflicts with my grandmother's "instructions" and ended up failing in his marriage.

This is a horrible example of what happens to families when a man does not leave his parents. According to the principle of covenant marriage, a man should leave his parents when he gets married! This also means that the parents must leave their sons. In particular, a man's mother must give her son independence in every way so that he can go completely to her daughter-in-law. Expecting a son to remain filial (i.e., dutiful to his parents) after marriage is not a biblical teaching, but a strict Confucian idea.

Confucianism emphasizes the union of children with their parents, even when they marry, so they cannot leave their parents for life. There are seven reasons why a wife can be divorced in Confucianism. The first is that she does not serve her in-laws well. Therefore, daughters-in-law should be extremely filial to their parents-in-law instead of uniting with their husbands.

Of course, children should be filial to both parents while they are married. But they shouldn't be filial to each parent to the detriment of the couple's union. There was once a couple who had been married for seven years, and the husband gave almost all of his salary to his parents. He never discussed this with his wife! It's basic common sense that when you get married, the first thing you should do is consult your spouse, yet some people lack that common sense.

The reason her husband's mindset is so hardened is because he never left his parents. Although he is physically gone, he is still emotionally tied to them. He is especially emotionally fused with his mother. What happens to one becomes what happens to the other. To borrow a term from the American psychiatrist Murray Bowen (1913-1990), her husband has a very low level of self-differentiation.[20] In other words, he is still dependent on his parents and unable to take the initiative to solve his own problems because he is not free from emotional interactions in his family of origin. These individuals usually have low self-esteem, are emotionally unstable, and act on emotions rather than rational thought.

Ironically, the more model children who have never disobeyed their parents since childhood, the more likely they are to do so. Why is this? Because they have been conditioned to unconditionally obey their parents' decisions at every turn, instead of solving their own problems, and have come to identify their feelings with those of their parents.

I actually had a couple like that. One day, a young man I had previously taught in a church brought a sister to me and introduced her to me as someone he was going to marry. I was so happy to bless them and watch them prepare for the wedding. But

★

20) F. B. Wichern, Sr., "Family Systems Therapy," in *Baker Encyclopedia of Psychology & Counseling*, ed. David G. Benner and Peter C. Hill, Baker reference library (Grand Rapids, MI: Baker Books, 1999), 444.

he confided in me that he couldn't understand her reaction as he prepared the wedding ceremony.

> Pastor, I really like it when my mother makes decisions, but my girlfriend doesn't seem to like it.

He didn't understand why she was having a hard time. He thought that if his parents liked it, she would like it, but that's just his own delusion. Her underlying psychology is that she wants her boyfriend to be independent of his parents from now on. At this point, he is in conflict with her. He has been a model student who has never disobeyed his parents before, and it is difficult for him to be in a strange situation where he has to "leave" his parents to listen to his girlfriend. Nevertheless, he must accept this unfamiliar situation from the bottom of his heart. In fact, the process of preparing for marriage is a man's gradual independence from his parents. At the same time, this means that the woman must do the same with her parents.

In any case, as the Bible teaches, the spouse, whether husband or wife, should be the first priority. Whenever I officiate at a wedding, there is a counsel I always give to the bride and groom.

> The groom should make the bride his top priority from now on.
> You really want to be independent of your parents. Likewise, the

bride should make the groom her top priority from now on.

In fact, it's an exhortation for both parents to listen to. Korean parents are very inclined to not let go of their children due to Confucianism. According to one expert, the percentage of parents over the age of 60 who still give their children pocket money and try to keep them in their arms is 8% in Japan, 11% in Hong Kong, and 83% in Korea.[21] That's a statistic I can agree with, given the percentage of marital problems I see in my practice.

That's why Christian parents must pay special attention to the Bible's teachings. If a man does not leave his parents, it is usually because his parents will not let him go. They worry excessively when their children marry and feel compelled to step in and solve any problems that arise. This may be tender parental love, but it may also be a distorted love that makes it impossible for the child to exist as an independent person before God.

Filial Piety Requires a Good Marriage

It may seem ironic, but the better the relationship between a

---

21) 황창연, "부부의 사랑", 「성필립보생태마을」(유튜브 채널), 2023년 4월 20일, https://youtube. com/shorts/-YQN7YRO_bg?si=-qLLcAA7lwMtx7Y1.

married couple, the more filial they are to their in-laws. Why is this? Because the energy of love that overflows between them will also flow to their in-laws. Because the Confucian tradition emphasizes the union of in-laws rather than the union of husband and wife, a married couple feels more like a son and daughter-in-law to their in-laws than a husband and wife. It's as if filial piety (i.e., duty to parents) is neglected when a couple has a good relationship.

But in reality, it's quite the opposite. The deep union of a couple is not a disrespect to parents, but a driving force for loving parents and filial piety. This is also my experience. When my wife and I were not getting along, I had no time to think about my mother and mother-in-law. But one day, when I was happy with my wife, I started thinking about how I could be better to my mother and mother-in-law. (Fathers on both sides passed away long before we got married, and now my mother is dead.) That is to say, when a man leaves his parents and unites with his wife, he becomes more filial to his parents.

This is the power of love that the union brings. If there is any anxiety on the part of our parents that their children will distance themselves from them because of the couple's union, it should be quickly dispelled. If a child marries and distances himself from his parents and cuts them off from the relationship, he either lacks basic humanity or has been seriously hurt by his parents. This is a different matter.

And the deep union of a married couple has a profound impact not only on the parents, but also on others as well. Especially pastors in church ministry should keep this in mind. The more conservative churches believe that if a pastor loves his wife too much, he will neglect his congregation, which is a typical Confucian mindset. This is because they want the union of the church members more than the union of the pastor and his wife. God wants the mystical union of Christ and the church to be witnessed through the union of husband and wife (Eph. 5:31-32). The deep union of a pastor and his wife, then, is an object lesson to the church members that demonstrates the mystical union of Christ and the church. Only when the pastor and his wife are happy and in love with each other can the church be truly happy.

This deep union goes far beyond the private dimension of the couple. Closer to home, it is an impulse for love and filial piety toward both parents and, more broadly, a means of witnessing to the relationship between Christ and the church to the community to which the couple belongs. In any case, love and happiness in Christ should overflow between the spouses.

 ## When a Man Does Not Unite with His Wife

According to Genesis 2:24, a married man should leave his

parents and unites with his wife. When a man marries, he is naturally united to his wife and they become one flesh. However, as mentioned earlier, they have become a married couple, but they need to become an actual couple. In other words, they have entered into the legal relationship of husband and wife, but they must live the actual relationship of husband and wife.

A couple's legal relationship is not destroyed unless they divorce. However, the legal relationship itself is not the actual union of the couple. Once a couple has entered into a legal relationship, they must stick together and become inseparable. As the Hebrew verb for "to join" (or "to unite") in Genesis 2:24 implies,[22] the couple should be stuck together at all times, as if soldered. It doesn't mean that they should be physically together attached 24/7, but that they should not live apart.

I was serving as an associate pastor at a church. I was in the ministry room after preaching at the Wednesday prayer service when my cell phone rang. As I pressed the call button, I began to hear sobbing. I panicked for a moment, but it sounded like something was going on, so I waited until she calmed down.

She introduced herself as Jessica, who has been married for 8 years. She said that she and her husband live far away from each other due to work. He works in Seoul and she works in the

---

*

22) See footnote 17.

countryside, and they have been living as a "monthly couple." They had an exemplary relationship before marriage, dreaming of a happy family, and even after their marriage, they shared God's Word every day. Although they were separated, they were coping well with the reality through the grace of His Word.

One day, she received a sharing message from her husband and realized that something was wrong. It was just devotional thoughts they usually shared, but she felt different that day. So, without telling her husband, she took the KTX (Korea Train Express) to Seoul at a late hour and rushed up to Seoul. When she opened the door to her apartment, she saw a woman's shoe on the doorstep. She tried to reassure herself that her mother-in-law had come, but when she opened the door to the bedroom, she saw something she should never have seen: a man and a woman with no clothes on!

Jessica was speechless again. As a pastor, I empathized and comforted her rather than giving her the right answer. I also cautiously advised her about the legal process ahead, but she knew much more than I did. She told me that she works at a divorce counseling center. She said that she deals with divorce cases all the time, so she could see so vividly what her husband had done and how he had done it that it upset her even more.

Pastor, I am all too familiar with the legal actions. I'm just wondering how to respond to God in this situation. I'm really hurting and it's so hard. But Pastor, do you think God is even alive?

Jessica's last words broke my heart. What did she mean when she said, "Do you think God is even alive?" Did she really react that way because she doubted God's existence? No, she didn't. She reacted that way because she knew that God was indeed alive, and she knew that God was always watching over her life.

In a slightly different context, recall how Peter reacted when Jesus was arrested and people questioned Peter. When they said, "You also were with Jesus of Galilee" (Matt. 26:69), he blurted out something he shouldn't have. He referred to Jesus as "the Man" and cursed and swore that he did not know Him (26:74). He then went outside and wept bitterly. This was not because Peter's faith had been destroyed or because he doubted Jesus' existence. Rather, he responded because he knew all too well who Jesus was and what He had done for him. A person who didn't know Jesus at all would never react like that. Why not? Because it has nothing to do with him.

Similarly, Jessica did not say such a thing because she doubted God's existence. She knew that God was indeed alive and watching over her life, so she reacted by asking, "Do you think God is even alive?" The question is, how can God remain still in such a situation?

At this point, we can make one observation. Jessica's crisis was caused solely by her husband's immoral behavior, not at all by God. No matter how painful it is, we should never blame God for such a situation. Of course, I never express such a preconceived notion during counseling. We must continue to comfort, encourage, and wait for the client to come to his/her own realization.

We can also see that irreparable wounds between a husband and wife greatly distort their view of God. This is because, as mentioned earlier, marriage and faith are connected in every aspect, and God has established the principle that the mystical union of Christ and the church is revealed through the union of husband and wife (Eph. 5:31-32). Therefore, a distorted relationship with your spouse will inevitably distort your relationship with God.

But we must not lose hope. Because our relationship with God can never be broken, even if our relationship with our spouse comes to an end (which it shouldn't!), we don't fall completely out of faith. To borrow a phrase from earlier, horizontal covenants can be broken, but vertical covenants are never broken.

No one can fully understand the bitterness of Jessica's heart after her husband irrevocably left her. I can only pray that God would give her the grace to recover. Thankfully, years later, she has overcome her wounds and her faith is stronger than ever. Although her husband left her for an adulteress, Jessica is living another life with Christ as her eternal Husband.

It is important to remember that irreparable damage can occur when a man is not rightly united with his wife. A husband and wife should strive to be united to each other. In other words, married couples shouldn't live apart, and if they do, it should be temporary. This is especially true after the honeymoon period, when love hormones take over. Husbands and wives should be united and enjoy an abundance of sexual intimacy as well as emotional intimacy.

When a Couple Doesn't Become One Flesh

I once went on a short-term mission trip to Mongolia with a group of young people. One day when I got back to the hostel, I checked my email and found a long message. I thought it was spam, so I was about to delete it. But when I looked at the sender's name, I realized that it was the name of a sister from my hometown.

> Pastor, how have you been? I know you're a little surprised by this unexpected email. But you're the only person I want to talk to about my marriage situation right now. We're a seemingly harmonious family, we're good believers in Jesus, and we seem to

have no problems. But since we got married, I'm starting to feel like he's not the same person I knew in our relationship, and that I've been cheated.

It was incredibly long, but I read it in one sitting, struck by her story. When I got back to Korea, I immediately contacted her and found out that the email was true, and we had a long counseling session. At the core of the couple's crisis was her husband's infidelity, which was unimaginable. A woman from the same church, whom he had known since before his marriage, and he had been having an inappropriate relationship and engaging in lewd behavior with each other for a long time. (I won't go into the details because it would be immoral.) Shockingly, she was a married woman with a child. She was a deaconess in the church with a reputation for good faith.

I had a hard time believing it even when I talked to her. It was hard for me to imagine that the good-hearted Jack (her husband) was the crazy man I had known before their marriage. But I couldn't doubt that it was true based on the evidence she showed me. However, there was one thing that I wondered about during our conversation, so I tenderly asked her how often they usually had sex.

In fact, I've hardly ever had it, except for the purpose of childbirth.

At that moment, I was a little shocked. It's amazing to me that a couple who had been married for only a few years was still sexless. They had not enjoyed sexual intimacy except for the purpose of childbirth, which was almost a state of asceticism.

The younger men are, the more likely they are to become sexually deviant, even if they're married, if their sexual needs go unfulfilled. Whether it's an actual affair or an internalized desire for another woman, it's easy to become sexually strayed. Of course, women are no exception. Married women, like the woman who committed adultery with Jack, are also surprisingly prone to sexual deviation.

That's why every married couple should enjoy sexual intimacy in abundance. Sexual communication between a married couple is a beautiful thing. You should often feel oneness with each other in the most secret and deepest intimacy, sharing your body and heart with all five senses. It's rare for a couple to be happy without sexual language and communication. Our God is pleased when couples are happy to share their sexuality with each other.

Going back to the story of Jack's wife, I have to point out one thing. You can't justify Jack's affair as if it was because of his wife's sexual abstinence. To say that her husband had no choice but to cheat because she wasn't actively engaged in their relationship is to kill her twice. There is no way to justify a husband's infidelity in that way. However, it is unfortunate that they did not communicate sexually as spouses.

Like women, men are more shy and awkward about expressing their desires than you might think. In Korean society, women feel as if they shouldn't express themselves sexually, and men associate sexual expression with a loss of pride if they are rejected. In reality, these are just social myths and prejudices, not principles of marriage. Many couples are not specifically taught this before they get married, so they continue to express themselves according to their old beliefs. Anyway, whether you're a husband or a wife, sharing your desires with someone other than your spouse is adultery, even if your spouse does not express himself or herself sexually. Under no circumstances should a person justify his/her infidelity by blaming it on his/her spouse's passivity.

Church Women Tamed by Asceticism

There are more women in the church who are tamed by asceticism than you might think. Of course, more and more young people and couples are finding the opposite to be true. There are still many middle-aged women who are not properly educated about sexuality at the time of marriage, which leads to many laughable situations.

There was a woman in a church who was in her late 40s. She and her husband were almost twelve years apart in age and had been married for over 20 years. Despite her parents' objections, they got married and were about to spend their first night together, but she was horrified. When she saw her husband undress and get on the bed, she was too scared to do anything. She went to her mom's house and told her about her problems, and after receiving detailed sex education, they started their marriage. Now they have a beautiful relationship.

Even among the young people in the church, I saw an ascetic sister. She was in her 30s and was the one I had taught before. She told me that she had never felt sexual desire in her life. Even when she was in a relationship with her boyfriend, she kept a strict physical distance. In addition, she had never seen an R-rated movie or video since she was a child. She had no interest in the natural way men and women touch each other in love or in sexual behavior after marriage. My wife and I were so concerned about her that we conducted a "special education" one day. I was somewhere else and my wife was watching a relatively low-key R-rated video with her. I still remember her telling me how shocked she was to see such a video when she was over 30 years old. Fortunately, she's now married to a wonderful man, has a happy family, and is doing well.

Another time, a woman in her 50s came to me after reading *A Theology of Dating*. She came to me for counseling because she was troubled by her son's love life. But no matter what she said, it was not a problem for young people today. I realized that her ascetic mindset was the bigger problem.

> Pastor, I was shocked when my son told me that he had a girlfriend, because I was in college and never dared to start a relationship. I got married because the missionary organization I worked for introduced me to a brother. I had never met the brother before, but I trusted the missionary. So I believed that if he introduced me to him, he must be a good person. That's why I married him. I didn't really have much love for him when I married him.

I wondered if she was "emotionally fused" with her son because she was shocked that he had a girlfriend, but fortunately, this was not the case. Her desire to see her son succeed in his independent life was evident throughout our conversation. However, she said that she really didn't understand how young people in the church could start dating casually. I kept telling her that it's not normal by her standards, but by the standards of today's young people, it was perfectly normal and even healthy.

It was only after we had talked for a while that she seemed

to realize how different her views were from those of her son's generation. It was the first time she realized that the standards and ways of previous generations, which she had held fast to as if they were biblical, might not be. In the eyes of today's church youth, their parents' generation is strictly ascetic. This is more true of the women of that era than of the men. This was evident in my conversation with my mother-in-law. When she was younger, she believed that expressing romantic feelings in church was a form of adultery. I remember when I was in middle and high school, church elders lectured us about how the chapel was not a "dating place."

God-Given, Beautiful Sexual Desire

Sexual desire is a physical response that makes a man and a woman long for each other. It's a gift from God that gives us a vivid sense of the couple's oneness through all five senses, so it's never impure or sinful. It's just that our spiritual perception of it is often distorted.

Church members who are accustomed to asceticism unwittingly perceive sexual desire as impure. I was one of them. There was a time in my middle school and high school years when my faith was at a fever pitch. I read and memorized the Bible with great fervor. One day, while reading the Song of Solomon, I got a bit of a shock.

> 3 Your lips are like a scarlet thread, and your mouth is lovely. Your cheeks are like halves of a pomegranate behind your veil. ... 5 Your two breasts are like two fawns, twins of a gazelle, that graze among the lilies. ... 11 Your lips drip nectar, my bride; honey and milk are under your tongue; the fragrance of your garments is like the fragrance of Lebanon. ... 15 a garden fountain, a well of living water, and flowing streams from Lebanon. (Song 4:3-15, ESV)

In Song of Solomon 4, Solomon sings about how beautiful his bride is. But the descriptions of women's bodies are very explicit. At the time, I really questioned how this could be in the Bible. It may be commonplace by today's standards, but it was enough to excite an adolescent boy 30 years ago. I wasn't just excited, I was sexually aroused. At the time, I was devastated to see myself reacting that way while reading the Bible. I condemned myself as an unscrupulous sinner for being sexually aroused by the Holy Bible.

Looking back, I realize that my ignorance of sexuality led to this. The Bible beautifully describes sexuality between a husband and wife. At the time, I thought that sexuality itself was impure. It was as if there shouldn't be any sexual content in the Bible. How could the Bible, God's holy Word, contain such impure content? I subconsciously thought that sexuality belonged to "evil" and not to the best, that it was only for survival and reproduction.

The premise of this idea is that sexuality came about as a result of humanity's transgressions. It assumes that sexuality is always sinful. But if you read the Bible as it is, there was sexuality before sin entered the world. The first transgression begins in Genesis 3, but before that, God created man, male and female, and told them to be fruitful and multiply (1:27-28). In order to be fruitful and multiply, they must have children through sexual union. Then, after the first human wedding, God said that the couple was united and became one flesh (2:24), which already includes sexual union accompanied by sexual desire. Sexuality, then, is something that God gave to humans before sin entered the world. Sexual desire has never been a result of sin.

How would sexual desire have been expressed in a sinless state? This is hypothetical, but we can make some educated guesses. In a sinless state, Adam and Eve would have felt God's presence so vividly that they would have perceived their marriage as a love triangle with God as the apex. If so, the first human couple would have been aware of God's presence when they expressed their sexual desires to each other, and would have done so with the utmost respect for each other. Even the sexual desires that caused them to crave each other would have been used as a means of worship to honor God.[23]

And, as Augustine argued, in the absence of sin, the sexual desire could have been controlled by reason. That is, the sexual desire was obedient to reason.[24] Perhaps the sense of perceiving the glory of God was extremely activated and powerful enough to control sexual desire. Sexual desire in itself is not sinful, but when it becomes so powerful that it causes us to crave each other without recognizing God, it immediately becomes a sin against God. Therefore, in a sinless state, sexual desire would have always obeyed Adam and Eve's reason.

Based on this, we should understand sexual desire as a beautiful gift from God. Couples whom God has brought into a covenant relationship are to express their sexual desire as if they were in a sinless state. Why is this? Because Adam and Eve in Eden is the lost original state of all couples. Therefore, Christian couples should express their sexual desires with the utmost respect for each other, recognizing God's presence. They should strive to make even the time they spend together a "bedroom worship" before God. They should also be able to control their sexual desires to the fullest extent of their reason so that their desires are not di-

★
23) John Piper, *This Momentary Marriage* (Wheaton, Illinois: Crossway Books, 2009), 121.
24) 배정훈 외, 『초대 교회와 마음의 치료』 (군포: 다함, 2022), 88.

rected toward anyone other than their spouse.

☖ Sexual Desire and Lust Are Different!

I once preached a Sunday sermon at a church in Busan. After the first and second services in the morning, I had a meal with the elders of the church, and the topic of *A Theology of Dating* came up. They mentioned their views on dating and marriage.

> Pastor, when we were married, there were times when we couldn't help but laugh. One couple we knew repented to God every night after having sex. They recognized that even sex between husband and wife was sinful.

It turns out that the elders of the church had been trained in college by a missionary organization that considered dating to be idolatry. Dating is idolatry? It's classic asceticism. Surprisingly, the atmosphere of that missionary organization has continued to this day. In fact, university students of the organization once "secretly" listened to my lecture at a church. After the lecture, they came to me and told me their problems.

> Pastor, that's actually what our missionary organization is still

teaching in a subtle way.

The missionary organization bases its teaching on Matthew 5:28, which reads "But I say to you that whoever looks at a woman to lust for her has already committed adultery with her in his heart." This is a misinterpretation because it equates "lust" in this verse with sexual desire. Lust means to "intentionally and perversely" harbor sexual desire for a specific object. In the context of the desire for sex, lust is included in sexual desire, but the two are by no means the same thing. The whole concept of sexual desire can be illustrated in the following diagram.

As you can see, we can categorize the concept of sexual desire into three main categories. The first is "marital passion" (A), which occurs in the relationship of a married couple. Next is "lust" (B), which is the desire for something other than the spouse. This

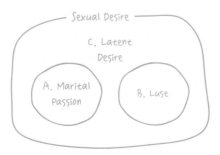

Three Concepts of Sexual Desire

includes such things as adultery, homosexuality, and pornography. Finally, there is "latent desire" (C), which is hidden in everyone, even if there is no specific object. It's a biological instinct for sex that is not usually expressed or manifested.

But extreme ascetics, such as the missionary organization mentioned above, consider not only B, but also A and C to be impure. For them, even the marital passion that arises in a conjugal relationship is perceived as sinful. Even the emotion of looking at the opposite sex and feeling beautiful is considered immoral before God.

However, Jesus condemned the state of lust (B), not both natural sexual desires (A and C), because it is God who endowed humans with sexual desire. As mentioned earlier, sexual desire was already present before sin entered the world. However, when sin entered the world, lust (B) was created among the sexual desires. This is a distorted sexual desire that is harbored or expressed toward an object other than the spouse to whom one is bound in marriage covenant before God.

To summarize, we must distinguish between sexual desire and lust. Sexual desire is a beautiful gift given to humans by God, and it is a blessed way for married couples to vividly feel their oneness with each other. This beautiful gift should not be perceived as something impure. The dangers of lust cannot be overemphasized, but we must never make the mistake of equating lust with sexual desire.

♥♥ Sexual Desire and Covenant

The sexual desire of a married couple is a sensual way of being faithful to the horizontal covenant of marriage. It is also interlocked with the vertical covenant with God. Let's revisit *The Triangle of Covenant* from earlier.

The Triangle of Covenant

Husband (H) and wife (W), who are in a horizontal covenant, are also in a vertical covenant with God. This is how every Christian couple exists before God. God has made a covenant of salvation with each of us in Christ (the vertical covenant), which is often expressed in the Bible as a marriage covenant between God and us.[25] Being in a spiritual marriage relationship with us, God has a holy desire for us. He tells us through the prophet Zephaniah how much He delights in us, His bride, and how much He loves us.

★

25) See footnote 4.

… He will rejoice over you with gladness, He will quiet *you* with His love, He will rejoice over you with singing." (Zeph. 3:17)

He even spoke in more explicit terms through the prophet Isaiah.

… And *as* the bridegroom rejoices over the bride, *So* shall your God rejoice over you. (Isa. 62:5)

In what way would a bridegroom delight in his bride? By longing for, desiring, and truly delighting in her with his whole being, accompanied by intense sexual attraction. This is how God delights in us. In other words, He delights in us and loves us, but not just on that level, but He "longs" for us in Christ and "desires" us with His whole being through the Holy Spirit. This is a holy desire directed toward us, His bride. This holy desire flows from the vertical covenant that husband and wife each have with God. God wants couples in a horizontal covenant relationship to imitate this holy desire and express it to each other. For this very purpose, God has endowed humans with sexual desire. So a couple's sexual desire is a mirror of God's holy desire. Therefore, the sexual desire should imitate holy desire as closely as possible to reflect the fullness of God's love.

For this to be accomplished, we must first be filled with holy desire for God. Just as God has a holy desire for us, a husband and wife must each maintain a spiritual state of holy desire and longing for God, because that is where the energy to desire each other lies. Of course, in the early days of the honeymoon, when they are full of love hormones, they desire each other intensely regardless of their spiritual state, but this desire is actually a state of sexual arousal due to the powerful hormonal secretion.

But this state has a shorter lifespan than you might think. After that, it is no longer possible to desire each other with the energy that comes from love hormones. So what should you do? Should you, like the people of the world, look for a new object to arouse your love hormones? Of course not! As mentioned earlier, a Christian couple is a love triangle with God as the apex, so they must find the energy to desire each other from God. With God's love poured out through the Holy Spirit, husbands and wives should train themselves to desire and long for each other. Then their sexual desire will begin to resemble God's holy desire.

🛏 Lust Is Idolatry

Again, sexual desire is a sensual way of being faithful to a covenant. This applies to both vertical and horizontal covenants. The holy desire is the vertical way to be faithful to the covenant with God, and the sexual desire is the horizontal way to be faithful to the covenant between a couple.

These holy and sexual desires are interlocked. No, they must always be interlocked. That is to say, a state of longing for God must be evidenced by a state of desiring for your spouse. In the early days of the honeymoon, when we are full of love hormones, we desire each other intensely, regardless of our desire for God. But as the hormones wear off, our desire for each other diminishes significantly. From this point on, you will desire your spouse with the same energy that you normally desire God.

This is where many couples get confused. They don't realize that if they don't desire their spouse, they don't desire God. I was one of them. Just as there is a state of being saved but not desiring God, there is often a state of being married but not desiring your spouse. The two are closely connected in every way: a vertical longing for God is expressed in a horizontal desire for a spouse.

Let's put it more simply. The more devout a couple is, the more sexually satisfied they are with each other. This has long been statistically proven in the United States. There are surveys that show that sexual satisfaction between couples is strongly related to their faith, and the more fervent their faith, the more likely they are to enjoy their sex life.[26] This may seem incompre-

★

26) 팀 라헤이 외, 『결혼행전』 김인화 옮김 (서울: 생명의말씀사, 2005), 9-10.

hensible to sex-averse ascetics, but it makes perfect sense to those who understand the beauty of sex as God created it.

The Bible describes the sex life of a married couple very beautifully. You'll find it in the Song of Solomon, as well as in the book of Proverbs.

> 15 Drink water from your own cistern, flowing water from your own well. 16 Should your springs be scattered abroad, streams of water in the streets? 17 Let them be for yourself alone, and not for strangers with you. 18 Let your fountain be blessed, and rejoice in the wife of your youth, 19 a lovely deer, a graceful doe. Let her breasts fill you at all times with delight; be intoxicated always in her love. (Prov. 5:15-19)

In this passage, the "cistern" and "well" are metaphors for a wife. In Song of Solomon, Solomon likens his bride to a "a spring locked, a fountain sealed" (4:12, ESV). Proverbs 5 exhorts husbands to "Drink water from your own cistern, flowing water from your own well." The "water" here represents the quenching of sexual desires.[27] In other words, to find satisfaction through sexual intercourse with their wives. Furthermore, "Let your fountain be blessed, … Let her breasts fill you at all times with delight; be

★
27) 브루스 월트키, 『NICOT 잠언 I』, 황의무 옮김 (서울: 부흥과개혁사, 2020), 359.

86

intoxicated always in her love." The idea is that husbands should admire their wives' physical bodies and find their sleep with her beautiful.

However, Proverbs 5 warns, "Let them be for yourself alone, and not for strangers with you." The idea is to preserve sexual purity between husband and wife. That is, your spouse should be the one who fulfills your sexual desires.

Now let's apply the analogy to our vertical relationship with God. As mentioned earlier, longing for God and desiring for our spouse are connected in many ways. A holy longing for God is demonstrated by a vigorous desire for one's spouse. If this still sounds strange to you, you have been tamed to a false asceticism. Many Bible scholars see the ultimate meaning of marital sex as representing the ultimate joy that exists between Christ and the church. John Piper even says, "The ultimate meaning of marital sex is about the final delights between Christ and his church."[28]

Marital sex is thus imbued with profound spiritual significance. Husbands and wives should recognize that the act of desiring and enjoying each other is a witness of the ultimate joy between Christ and us that will be experienced in the future. In this context, a married couple's lovemaking is a "bedroom worship," a whole-body expression of their longing for God.

★

28) John Piper, *This Momentary Marriage*, 127.

So what happens to a couple when they stop desiring their spouse? This goes beyond just being estranged, because when a couple does not desire each other sexually and enjoy satisfaction, they are ultimately not enjoying the joy between God and themselves. In this state, it is very likely that the husband or wife is secretly lusting after someone other than their spouse. As sexual beings, we are constantly looking for objects to express our sexual desire unless it is extinguished.

The moment the same sexual desire is expressed toward an object outside of the covenant relationship of marriage, it immediately turns into lust. (See the whole concept of sexual desire as introduced on Page 80.) This means sexual deviation. But the problem is not just that we are sexually deviant from our spouse. Why is this? Our sexual desire based on our horizontal covenant with our spouse is a reflection of our holy desire based on our vertical covenant with God. In other words, sexual desire between a couple is a way of revealing the holy desire between God and us.

Therefore, to be sexually deviant from one's spouse is to be spiritually deviant from God. Again, this is because one's spiritual state of longing for God is evidenced by desiring for one's spouse. Therefore, married couples must remember that lust is idolatry and strive to desire each other. They must train themselves to desire each other on a different level than the sexual desire based on love hormones that arises spontaneously in the newlywed stage.

Husbands and wives must be filled with the Holy Spirit, for it is the "fullness of the Spirit" that causes us to love and desire God (see Rom. 5:5).

Experience Holy Affection

As mentioned earlier, the average romantic period during which a married couple is filled with love hormones and desires each other is about two years. After that, they continue to desire each other, but it depends much more on the will to love than on the emotion of love. In other words, rather than the passionate love of newlyweds, they naturally and willingly desire each other out of courtesy and consideration for each other. Since the will to love is based on the marriage covenant, husbands and wives must have the will to desire each other unless the marriage is broken.

The problem is that sometimes the loving will to desire each other does not arise. There are many reasons for this. Your spouse may have committed a serious wrong and hurt your feelings, or you may have health problems that prevent you from having any desire. If this is not the case, you should check your spiritual state.

As we often say, Christian marriage is a triangle with God as the apex. Not just any triangle, but a *covenantal triangle* with God as the apex. The vertical and horizontal covenants interlock to form an unbreakable relationship between God and the husband and wife. Within this covenantal framework, God has set up an interlocking cycle of holy desire with Him and sexual desire between the couple. In addition to *The Triangle of Covenant* introduced earlier, here is another diagram.

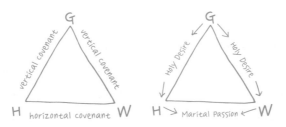

The Structure of Covenant and Sexual Desire

Once the expiration date of the love hormone is over, a husband and wife can desire each other with the same energy that they normally desire God. Of course, they may not desire God and may do so "willingly" on a general level. However, it is more likely to be a feeling of obligation or compulsion to do so as a spouse rather than a desire from the heart, because the love hormones are not being secreted, and the effort is simply willed without any emotions of love. Women are usually more likely to recognize this than men. No matter how much a husband buys his wife gifts and tries to satisfy her in bed, if it doesn't come from the heart, it doesn't feel soulful to her.

In this state, neither husband nor wife can desire their spouse with their own strength. That is why you need God's love poured out from above. This love is manifested in proportion to the degree to which one normally desires God.

At this point, we need to remind ourselves again of where love comes from. The Bible testifies that God is love, and that this love is manifested in the fact that God sent His only begotten Son into the world so that we might live, and that He sent Him as a propitiation for our sins (1 John 4:8-10). In other words, God's love is manifested in the event of the cross, and this is the source of the love that is poured out on us.

Therefore, couples whose love hormones are past their expiration date should work on realizing God's love as shown on the cross. If you're still wondering what God's love has to do with marital love, reread *Loving God & Loving Spouse* on page 21. A husband or wife who is filled with God's love can rightly love and rightly desire his/her spouse. They will desire each other's bodies and hearts with a different kind of love than the love hormones used to produce.

To be filled with God's love, we must frequently use the means of grace: the Word and prayer. A powerful outward evidence of our love for God is our closeness to His Word. Why is this? Because we cannot separate the object of our love from his/her word. If one were to say to his/her beloved, "I love you, but I don't want to be close to your words," who would accept his/her confession of love as true? Husbands and wives should diligently seek to be close to God's Word and hunger for His love. They should ask for the Holy Spirit's help to keep their hearts burning with love for God. This in itself is already an act of prayer.

God's grace is "infused" into us with the help of the Holy Spirit through the Word and our prayer.[29] To be infused with grace means that something from God enters into our being. There is something invisible that affects our whole person that enables us to love God. We don't necessarily have to think of this as a special experiential phenomenon. Christians usually experience that their hearts are touched and filled spiritually when they are spiritually exhausted, reading the Bible one day, or hearing an acquaintance speak from the Bible.

I refer to this phenomenon as God infusing us with a *holy affection*. It is God's grace that enables us to love God. The more often you experience this grace, the more passionately you love God. This creates an energy of love within you that drives you to love your spouse like never before. Whereas before you loved your spouse in a state of sexual arousal that comes from love hormones, now you love your spouse in a state of spiritual arousal that comes from God.

★

29) See the answer to Q. 77 in the Westminster Shorter Catechism.

This is where you can have a truly mystical experience. When you are filled with spiritual arousal, you are also sexually aroused toward your spouse. To put it more bluntly, when you are filled with the Holy Spirit, you are filled with sexual desire. In this case, we're not talking about lust, but sexual desire between a married couple. Since the sensory functions of the body are generally more active when filled with the Holy Spirit, the sexual function tends to be more active as well. That's why, as we mentioned earlier, the more devout couples are, the more sexually satisfied they are.

In fact, this is my experience as well. I often feel God's love with all my five senses. I think it is because of my experiential disposition in faith. Especially when I pray by memorizing the Bible, my whole body often feels a holy tremor, and I feel as if God's love is being vividly poured into my whole person. That is to say, I often experience the presence of the Holy Spirit.[30] At this time, I feel a strong holy affection in my whole person. I often wish that this time of being filled with God's love could just stop. Oddly enough, this state of spiritual arousal makes me desire for

★

30) The word *presence* refers to God's manifestation of Himself in our time and space. Of course, in general, the Holy Spirit is present to all Christians because God is with His people (covenantal presence), but this article refers to an exceptional phenomenon of presence that is different from the norm. 존 프레임, 『존 프레임의 조직신학』 김진운 옮김 (서울: 부흥과개혁사, 2017), 61-63.

my wife even more. Whereas before, under the control of love hormones, I focused on satisfying my own needs, I now think about how I can satisfy my wife's body and and heart with the love God is pouring into me.

This is the actual enjoyment of the covenantal triangle mentioned earlier. The holy desire between God and me is actually a virtuous cycle in which the holy desire is intertwined with the sexual desire within the covenantal framework. The holy affection that God infuses does not stay between me and God, but flows to my spouse in a horizontal covenant relationship. Therefore, the more often married couples experience the holy affection, the more sexually enriched they will be. And the sexual fulfillment that they enjoy is in turn expressed in holy longing for God, which means that together they love God passionately, are sensitive to His Word, and pray fervently.

1. Name the three elements of covenant marriage and briefly describe each one.

2. Are there any areas of your relationship that you struggle with because your spouse hasn't been able to leave his/her parents? If so, discuss them openly with each other.

3. How often do you currently have sexual communication with your spouse? Do you actually believe that sexual desire between a couple is a beautiful gift from God? If not, why not?

4. Do you want to be more filled with God's love in order to desire your spouse? How are you specifically working on loving God passionately?

CHAPTER 4

Upgrading Marital Love

🕯 How to Overcome Christian Boredom

All couples experience boredom, to varying degrees. The dictionary definition of *boredom* is "the state of being weary and restless through lack of interest."[31] The word is used in many contexts, but when applied to married couples, it can be defined as a lack of sexual attraction to one's partner and a feeling of weariness toward him/her.

There's a recent survey on marital boredom. Duo, a marriage information company, surveyed 500 married men and women between the ages of 20 and 39 and found that 65.4% of respondents had experienced boredom.[32] This percentage is likely due to newlyweds or young couples, but if we extend it to middle-aged couples in their 40s and beyond, it's safe to say that all couples go through boredom, big or small. What's more, once we get through a period of boredom, it doesn't mean it's over. Couples who have been married for a long time know from experience what it's like.

Biologically, it's natural for couples to experience boredom. No matter how sexually attracted you are when you're newlyweds, as you get used to each other and the sexual act becomes re-

---

31) Merriam-Webster, "boredom," accessed January 10, 2025, https://www.merriam-webster.com/dictionary/boredom.

32) 오상훈, ""배우자가 이유 없이 짜증난다"... 부부 10명 중 6명 겪는 '권태기' 극복 비결 물어보니", 『헬스조선』, 2024년 4월 17일, https://health.chosun.com/site/data/html_dir/2024/04/16/2024041602351.html.

petitive, sexual pleasure diminishes because the same stimuli over and over again decreases the secretion of dopamine in your brain.

At this point, we realize that our emotional state of love for our spouse is not the same as before. Your spouse realizes that your feelings and emotions are not the same as before. In the survey mentioned above, the most common symptom of boredom was "I get annoyed with my spouse for no reason."

It's strange, isn't it? Apparently, at the beginning of a relationship or marriage, he/she was loving and attractive for no reason, and then a few years into the marriage, they react to each other as "annoying for no reason." I've seen couples break up because they think their love for each other has changed and they don't love each other anymore. There have even been cases of people divorcing because of the way they squeeze their toothpaste or take out the garbage. Believe it or not, this is a true story from a divorce lawyer.[33]

This phenomenon between married couples is no exception for Christians. Christians and non-Christians are not biologically different. However, we have a divine power source that allows us to overcome marital boredom. Of course, there are many couples in the world who overcome boredom and restore their relationship.

★

33) 유경상, "이혼 변호사 최유나 "살인자 피고 무서워, 치약·분리수거 탓 이혼 많아"", 『뉴스엔미디어』, 2022년 10월 26일, https://www.newsen.com/news_view.php?uid=202210260532061710#google_vignette.

But they find the power to overcome boredom within themselves. Or they learn from other couples who have already overcome it. The same is true of the boredom busters in the above survey.

① Understanding through honest conversation (27.7%)

② Time will tell (14.5%)

③ Creating time together (10.4%)

④ Positive mindset (9.8%)

⑤ Take time for yourself (8.7%)

As you can see, all of the answers are either some kind of internal drive or temporary distance. Also, the biggest help in overcoming boredom is "having a friend who has a good marital love." In summary, non-Christian couples either rely on some kind of internal drive to overcome boredom, or they seek advice from couples they know who have already overcome it.

Of course, these methods are still valid for Christian couples. We should strive to understand each other through honest communication, make time for each other often, have a positive mindset, and be accepting and caring. We should also frequently seek wise counsel from couples we know who have already made it through.

But there's one thing missing: the love of God that has united us as husband and wife. Again, the Christian couple is a love triangle with God as the apex. We need to remember that the couple's love is based on God. To say that a couple is in a boredom is the exact opposite of saying that they fell in love when they first met. When they fell in love, the "love" they experienced was a state of sexual arousal caused by the secretion of *dopamine*.[34] It's a biological, chemical reaction in the body, and it's always temporary. This means that there will always come a point in time when the period of falling in love will wear off. This is when we enter the so-called boredom phase. Of course, it's a stretch to define any period of time without the secretion of love hormones as a boredom phase. But in contrast to the initial state of love in the beginning of a relationship, a couple's marriage is a series of small and large boredom phases.

Fortunately, Christian couples have a special way to overcome marital boredom. They can fill the void left by their depleted love hormones with God's love poured out from above! I've already explained how this is possible on theological grounds in the previous article. The love we create, no matter how noble, must have an expiration date. Whether it is the biological secretion of love hormones, or the spiritual and metaphysical love that is not physical.

But there is no end to God's love poured out from above. The bored Christian couple must now become hungry for this love.

★

34) In addition to *dopamine*, other love hormones include *oxytocin*, *endorphins*, and *phenyleth-ylamine*.

Whereas before they thought they could love each other with their own love, they have now realized that it is impossible. When they were newlyweds, they may have thought they were loving each other with God's love. To a certain extent, this is true. It doesn't make sense for siblings who know God's love to love each other and not have any of it.

But during that time, they were unknowingly in a state of sexual arousal that was more a biological response than a love of God. This in itself is not a bad thing at all. God is the one who gave us our sexual desire. It's just a problem that our senses for recognizing this state are not perfect, and we fall into the illusion that this romantic period will (or should) last forever. But God frees us from that illusion. Because He knows our weakness in recognizing sexual arousal as "holy," and because He knows that if it continues, we will become slaves to our sexual desires, He takes it away for us.

God then induces the bored couple to long for Him. Since God is at the apex of *The Triangle of Love*, as the husband and wife each draw closer to God, their relationship can grow closer to each other.[35] At this point, the husband and wife regain the energy to love each other again. This is because they realize that the source of the love that exists between them is not themselves, but

★

35) See *A Triangle with God as the Apex* on page 33.

God. And it is at this moment that they realize another truth: the reason they have become bored and reacted to each other as "annoying for no reason" is because they do not love God rightly.

Couples who are in a boredom phase should take a serious look at themselves. They should honestly ask themselves if they really love God as they should, and if there has been a "spiritual boredom" between them and God. When a person is filled with God's love, that love is so intense that when they look at their spouse, they see them as God sees them in Christ. In other words, just as God looks at us in Christ as if we were the righteous who have not sinned, even though we are still sinners, so the husband and wife who have fallen in love with Him look at each other just as God looks at us.

However, in my counseling practice, I have observed that couples in boredom are already alienated from God's love. Because their relationship with God, the source of love, is already broken, they immediately fall into boredom because they are no longer releasing dopamine toward their spouse. This was actually my condition 12 years ago. At that time, I didn't realize that I was in a workaholic state and tried to ignore my boredom with my wife. Later I realized that I was already in a state of spiritual boredom, alienated from God's love. To this day, I often diagnose my condition by recalling that terrible experience.

Therefore, in order to overcome boredom, big or small, Christian couples must first of all be filled with God's love. They must honestly admit that they are no longer able to love their spouse with their own energy, and they must resolve to love rightly in God from now on. They may still be annoyed with their husbands and angry with their wives, but they should endure it for God's sake and pray hard to be filled with His love. If you don't have the will to do this, and you don't even want to think about it, I would seriously advise you to seek professional counseling, because this is a serious problem for a Christian couple.

Perhaps the reason why every couple experiences boredom, big or small, is His providence to make us realize that our hope in life is in Him. Strangely enough, when you deeply realize this, your spouse suddenly seems lovable. This is because your inner sphere, which you were trying to fill with your spouse's love, is now filled with God's love. In this state, you can love your spouse like never before. The bottom line is that you can love your spouse again and overcome boredom only when you are properly grounded in God's love.

Defining the Concept of Overcoming Boredom

Non-Christians also have a suggestion for overcoming boredom. It is to realize that love is not just the emotion of passionate love.[36] This is a fact that I emphasize repeatedly in *A Theology of Dating* when dealing with the concept of love. In addition to the emotional component, there is a strong element of will in love. And it is very important to understand the relationship between the two correctly. In this article, I would like to summarize the concept of love in its entirety. Even married couples often go through life without knowing what love is.

As I argue in *A Theology of Dating*, the existential definition of love is "God is love."[37] That is, God's very existence is love. Conversely, we hesitate to say "love is God" because it can be misunderstood as if the concept of love itself is God. In that case, as C. S. Lewis pointed out, if love becomes God, it becomes the demon.[38] Rather, love should be understood as an existential attribute of God.

Therefore, those who realize God's existence and "know" God also know what love is, "for love is of God" (1 John 4:7). At this point, every Christian couple should constantly examine their love. They should frequently examine where their love for their spouse is based. Reconnect with the awareness that you love your husband or wife with the love that belongs to God because you

---

★

36) 오상훈, ""배우자가 이유 없이 짜증난다"... 부부 10명 중 6명 겪는 '권태기' 극복 비결 물어보니", https://health.chosun.com/site/data/html_dir/2024/04/16/2024041602351.html.

37) Ryul J. Kwon, *A Theology of Dating*, 50-53.

38) C. S. Lewis, *The Four Loves* (New York: Harcourt, Brace and Company, 1960), 17.

love God. At the very least, if you consider yourself a Christian, you should recognize that marital love is impossible without God.

Given the premise of existential love ("God is love"), we can also express love conceptually: "love is an operation of the will accompanied by emotion."[39] This is a conceptualization of love that reveals the relationship between the two components that formally make up love: will and emotion.

In focusing primarily on "dating" before marriage *A Theology of Dating* has not yet fully explored the will and emotion that arises from the love between a husband and wife, i.e., the covenant relationship of marriage. It has been limited to discussing the will and emotion of love in general, without elaborating on how the roots of the will and emotion are formed and how they influence each other. Now, in keeping with the title of this book, *A Theology for Married Couples*, we will focus on marriage and give it a more three-dimensional treatment.

In formal aspect, love is neither an emotion nor a will. People who understand love as an emotional state attach too much significance to the secretion of love hormones and constantly seek the symptoms of love, such as excitement for the opposite sex, heart palpitations, and overwhelming longing. However, married couples soon experience that these physical manifestations fade

★

39) Ryul J. Kwon, *A Theology of Dating*, 57.

away. From this point on, the husband and wife notice a change in their view of love, which means that they naturally realize that there are other factors at play in their love besides the emotional state caused by hormonal secretions.

Of course, this is not the case for some couples. They assume that their love has changed because their emotional state is not the same as it used to be, and they assume that they are in a boredom phase. They try to overcome the boredom phase, and their idea of overcoming the boredom phase is to return the emotional state of love to its previous state. But this is biologically impossible. Sure, you can regain some of the excitement and sexual craving you once had, but you can't get back to the same state of falling in love when you first met.

Therefore, we must properly define the concept of overcoming boredom. When we say that a Christian married couple overcomes boredom, we mean that they still maintain the will to love, even when the emotional state of love is not the same as before. The specific way to do this is to understand exactly where the will to love is held and to strengthen it. The point that holds the will to love is the "covenant" of marriage, as mentioned earlier. This covenant has two dimensions: vertical and horizontal. We've already covered this in detail. The horizontal covenant between husband and wife is interlocked with the vertical covenant between each of them and God. So, while the horizontal covenant is the primary point at which the will to love is rooted between a husband and wife, the final point is the vertical covenant with God, which is also God Himself. This can be illustrated as follows:

As shown in the illustration, the will to love is the lower, invisible part of the ground. The emotion of love, on the other hand, is the upper, visible part of the ground. This is easy to understand with common sense. The emotional state of love is easily recognized by the couple because it's visible in their facial expressions

The Structural Diagram of Love and Covenant

and tone of voice. On the other hand, the will to love is not so obvious, so it takes a serious conversation between the two of you to know exactly how you feel. We've talked in detail about what the will to love is between a couple in the previous section.[40]

Now let's look at where the will to love is rooted. It is based primarily on the horizontal covenant between husband and wife, which is currently assumed to be in a state of boredom, meaning that there is no sexual desire between the couple. This sexual desire is also intertwined with a holy desire for God,[41] so the couple must each check their level of desire for God. As we argued earlier, once the love hormones are exhausted, you can desire your spouse with as much energy as you normally desire God. At this point, if the desire for God does not arise at all, the couple should examine their own spiritual state. In other words, if there is no holy desire for God, based on the vertical covenant, then his/her boredom stems from spiritual boredom. He/she doesn't want to desire his/her spouse because his/her relationship with God is not good and God's love is not in his/her heart. At this point, many couples are reluctant to have an honest conversation. They keep trying to tell themselves that they still love God, but they don't like their spouse. But this is not true.

★

40) See *What Is the Will to Love Between a Couple?* on page 41.

41) See pages 84-94.

Again and again, love for God is demonstrated through love for one's spouse. Not just any love, but a level of desire for the whole person. This doesn't mean just having a peak state of sexual arousal like when you're a newlywed. After a few years of marriage, everyone realizes that this is impossible. It's not about returning to the hormonal state of love that you had before.

In conclusion, the correct concept of overcoming boredom is to be captivated by God's holy affection and to keep the will to love unchanged without being swayed by the emotional state of love. We will see what this means in the next article.

🕯️ Distinguishing Affection from Emotion

The phrase *holy affection* appears many times in this book. It originally appeared in *The Religious Affections* by Jonathan Edwards (1703-1758). He defined affections as "the more vigorous and sensible exercises of the inclination and will of the soul."[42] The term *holy affection*, then, can be understood as a prominent activity of the soul's inclination and will in relation to God. This is because the attribute "holy" is always associated with God.

The will to love is rooted in the covenant, but the power that

★

42) 조나단 에드워즈, 『신앙과 정서(개정역판)』 서문강 옮김 (서울: 지평서원, 2009), 35.

sustains it is in the holy affection. This is distinct from mere emotion. Affection and emotion may seem similar at first glance, but they differ in many ways. The following table summarizes them:

Affection	Emotion
• An exercise of mind, involving the inclination and will of the soul.	• A physical feeling that responds to stimuli without inclination or will.
• Includes emotion, but is a much broader concept.	• A concept that is included in affection, but can stand alone.
• Has a continuous attribute.	• Has a temporary attribute.

The Difference Between Affection and Emotion

As the table shows, affection involves the inclination and will of our soul and is also an exercise of the mind. Thus, affection includes emotion, but it is a much broader concept and does not depend on emotional states. This is why it has a continuous attribute. As long as it is connected to God, it is *holy* affection, and as long as it is possessed by the Holy Spirit, it will never be extinguished.

Emotion, on the other hand, is a physical sensation that reacts to a stimulus without the inclination or will of our soul. For example, when you touch a heated piece of metal, you automatically and involuntarily feel the heat. This feeling is not accompanied by any inclination or will. Therefore, emotion is a concept that can exist independently of affection. Of course, when affection becomes intense, it includes an emotional state. Also, because emotion is a physical sensation or feeling that responds to a stimulus, it doesn't last and it has a temporary attribute. That is, it disappears when the stimulus is no longer present.

A diagram of the relationship between affection and emotion is shown below (right), which is virtually identical to the *Existential Love vs. Conceptual Love* diagram discussed in *A Theology of Dating.*[43]

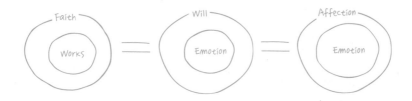

The Relationship Between Affection and Emotion

Thus, this leads to the conclusion that affection and will are the same, and they are. Edwards also says that affection is essentially indistinguishable from will.[44] The distinction is that affection is a much more intense and energetic state than will. So the realm of emotion embedded in it is much larger in the case of affection

★
43) Ryul J. Kwon, *A Theology of Dating*, 66.
44) 조나단 에드워즈, 『신앙과 정서(개정역판)』 36.

than in the case of will, which is to say that the emotion embedded in affection is an emotional state elevated to a higher level. To explain further, on a general level, the emotion of love derived from the will of love can be said to be close to a state of sexual arousal. And the emotion of love derived from the holy affection can be said to be close to a state of spiritual arousal, which includes a state of sexual arousal, and further longing for God.

Because *A Theology of Dating* focuses on the dating stage before marriage, the will and emotion of love are treated at a general level. Since the couple has not yet developed into a covenant relationship, it was deemed premature to fully address the covenant-rooted will to love. In this book, *A Theology for Married Couples*, the will to love is now treated in a holistic and three-dimensional way in the form of "holy affection" in connection with the covenant. This is because I am convinced that the will to love that exists between a husband and wife must eventually be fully sublimated into a holy affection toward God. This is the point at which a couple who constantly cultivates it can properly overcome boredom.

Now, let's be more specific and apply this to unmarried couples: the will to love is much more susceptible to the emotion of love because the will doesn't yet have a covenant that is rooted in it. In addition, the secretion of love hormones, which is directly related to the emotional state, is in full swing at this time, making the will to love even more unstable depending on the hormonal state. As you can see from the diagram above, in principle, the will to love is a more comprehensive concept than emotion, so it shouldn't be variable depending on emotional states. However, there is no covenant that holds the will to love, so in practice, there is always the possibility that the will to love can be extinguished depending on the emotional state of love.

But it's different for a married couple. The will to love is now fully rooted in the covenant. Therefore, the will to love cannot be extinguished by emotional states. The problem is that the emotion of love is not what it used to be. In a married relationship, the will to love is not extinguished by emotion because of the covenant, but it is greatly affected by the emotional state. Since the dopamine secretion is not as high as it used to be, the love that is inherent in a couple is slowly fading away, and this is when they start to feel bored with each other. In addition, the lack of communication between couples due to busy work schedules or childcare issues can prolong and intensify the boredom.

This is when Christian couples should pray and desperately seek for a "holy affection" to come between them. Of course, in times of boredom, it is tempting not to want to create such a situation, or even to deliberately avoid it. However, you must do everything in your power to beat your stubborn heart into submission so that you can experience another level of love together from now on! You must honestly admit that you can no longer love your spouse with the strength inherent in you, and you must seek the help of the Holy Spirit, because God's love is poured in our hearts through the Holy Spirit (Rom. 5:5).

As already mentioned, this is infused into us by the grace of the holy affection. At this point, we experience the renewal of the will to love. Our will has been greatly influenced by the emotion of love that comes from the state of sexual arousal, but now we feel that our will is controlled by the holy affection that comes from the state of spiritual arousal and is no longer greatly influenced by our emotional state. From this point on, we realize that it is not our will to love that controls the emotion of love, but the holy affection that God gives me. Therefore, the holy affection is a form of the will to love elevated to a higher level. Entering into this state is how Christian couples overcome boredom.

Holy Affection and the Emotion of Love

Now let's look at the relationship between holy affection and the emotion of love in the three diagrams above. As argued in detail in *A Theology of Dating*, this relationship corresponds exactly to the relationship between faith and works. In salvation, faith is a concept that includes works and is the cause of works, and works are the result of faith, meaning that a true believer in Jesus must demonstrate his faith through evangelical works.

The will and the emotion of love are related in this way. The will to love is a concept that includes the emotion and is the cause of the emotion, and the emotion of love is the result of the will. Of course, the emotion of love experienced during the premarital period is often unrelated to the will, because it is mainly a state of intense sexual arousal due to the secretion of dopamine. Furthermore, the will to love is not yet fully rooted, so it is difficult to establish a complete causal relationship.

So the exact counterpart to the relationship of faith and works is the will and emotion of love that exists between a couple after marriage. This correspondence is inevitable because God's covenantal love is applied to us for salvation (faith and works) and that covenantal love is applied to married couples (covenant relationship).[45] As mentioned earlier, the will to love in marriage is greatly influenced by our emotional state, so it is essential for Christian couples to have a holy affection that elevates their love to a higher level. From this point on, the will to love is influenced more by the holy affection that God gives than by our emotional state. The will to love can then function fully as the cause of emotion. This is because the will to love is held by God's love and

★

45) For a more detailed discussion, see *A Theology of Dating*, 64–69.

manifests as a holy affection, and at the same time, at this point, the emotional state of loving one's spouse is formed. So the will to love is not essentially distinct from the holy affection. There is only a difference in intensity and vigor.

The relationship between faith and works, then, corresponds exactly to the relationship between holy affection and the emotion of love. That is, the holy affection is the concept that includes the emotion of love and is the cause of the emotion, and the emotion of love is the result of the holy affection. Of course, the emotion of love that are formed at this time are completely different from those formed primarily in the state of sexual arousal before. Because it is a holy affection that is poured out through the Holy Spirit, the emotion of love that results from it is expressed in the direction of further longing and desiring God (i.e., the state of spiritual arousal), including the state of sexual arousal. Previously, when the dopamine secretion was high, longing for God and desiring one's spouse were somehow thought of as conflicting concepts, but now, mysteriously, the emotion of love flows out and is expressed in such a way that one can desire one's spouse and still long for God even more. In this context, the fullness of the Holy Spirit and the fullness of sexual desire in a couple are proportional, because the state of passionately loving God is the fullness of the Holy Spirit, and the state of wholly desiring one's spouse is the fullness of sexual desire, and the two go hand in hand.

This is a state that only married couples can enjoy. In pre-marital relationships, the fullness of the Holy Spirit and the fullness of sexual desire cannot continue in proportion because the couple is not yet united and has not entered into a covenant relationship. Moreover, the sexual desire formed at this time is almost a product of sexual arousal, and it is not sufficient to fully recognize God. Sexual desire must be controlled by God's holy affection if it is to have its proper place and function. Sexual desire, which is merely the result of sexual arousal, is often independent of the will to love, leading to frequent attempts to engage in inappropriate romantic behaviors that have nothing to do with God's holy affection. They are even more exposed to this danger during pre-marital dating, and even after marriage, if they are not controlled by the holy affection, they will attempt such dangerous provocations toward the opposite sex.

The emotion of love, then, must be the result of the will. The emotion of love should flow not from a mere will to love, but from a holy affection toward God. We must strive in many ways to ensure that this emotional state is expressed in abundance toward our spouse. Otherwise, we may come to a point where our emotion will be directed toward the opposite sex.

To illustrate this principle, let's use the previous diagram. Delete the outer part of the diagram and present it simultaneously on the right.

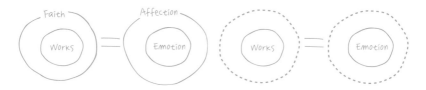

The Relationship Between Faith and Works, Affection and Emotion

In the diagram on the left, the relationship between faith and works, affection and emotion, is fully formed. Just as the Christian's works flow from saving faith, so the Christian couple's emotions flow from holy affection. There is no need to think of this state as a special case. All believers in Jesus exhibit evangelical works, only in varying degrees. Similarly, a Christian couple may find that when their dopamine levels are not as high as they used to be, they are willing to endure in order to express their emotion of love toward their spouse for the sake of God. This general state is called the *will and emotion of love*, while the state of being filled with love for God and having an intense emotion of love for one's spouse is called the *holy affection and emotion of love*. In any case, Christians live their lives in the state of the diagram on the left, with only a difference in degree.

But what would happen if we were in the state shown in the diagram on the right? How would we react if the faith and affection that control our works and emotions were extinguished? All people, whether saved or unsaved, exhibit works and emotions.

Non-Christians express their works from a general moral conscience and their emotions of love from the affection (or will) they generate from their inherent power. By way of illustration, their state is as shown in the diagram on the right. When they believe in Jesus and are born again, the source of their works and emotions changes. They are now God-related works and God-related emotions, respectively. This is the state shown in the diagram on the left.

Now let's continue the argument from the relationship between faith and works by focusing on holy affection and the emotion of love. The emotion of love itself is neutral, but when the framework that controls it is removed, it is sometimes hard to know which way it will go. We think we're in control of our emotions, but when we think about it, we realize that in many cases we're not. We like to think of ourselves as rational beings with logic and rationality, but in reality, we're controlled and influenced by our emotions in far more situations than we realize. No matter how right you are, or how bad you are, if you get caught doing something wrong, it's hard to accept it when your feelings (or emotions) are hurt.

So we have to train ourselves to control and manage our emotions. This is especially true when it comes to the emotion of love between a man and a woman. Before marriage, we have all experienced that a special emotional state wells up within us at the sight of a person of the opposite sex. *A Theology of Dating* explains in detail that although this emotional state is very precious, we should not conclude that such a state is love. Why is this? Because in love, in addition to the element of emotion, there is a strong element of will. This will to love began to strengthen and take root, and we became a couple who entered into the covenant relationship of marriage.

Now the emotion of love that we express is not infinitely free in and of itself, but is controlled by the covenantal framework of the will to love (or holy affection). As mentioned earlier, the intense and vigorous form of the will to love is the holy affection, which originate from God. Therefore, to say that the holy affection is extinguished is to say that we are left in a situation where our emotion of love is uncontrolled and unlimited.

We are very vulnerable to the emotional state of love in our relationships with men and women. Unless our sexual desire is completely extinguished, we all have an instinct to crave the opposite sex and express our emotions of love towards him/her. Even if it doesn't lead to an actual sexual act, we still want to express our emotions and our hearts in some way. This is not an exception, even for Christians.

This is where the holy affection plays a very important role. It exerts a strong control over the emotion of love, keeping it in place and directed only toward your spouse. But what happens if you yourself allow the holy affection to dissipate? What happens if you continue to allow yourself to be in an emotional state of love without a framework, as shown in the diagram on the right? Over time, you may find that your emotions are inclined toward the opposite sex, not your spouse. You may even recognize that you are in such a state and, strangely enough, not consider it a sin, because the holy affection that makes you aware of God has already been extinguished.

At this point we see again that loving our spouse and loving God are interlocked. A married couple cannot rightly love their spouse unless they fully love God, because the emotions of love they express toward their spouse are controlled by the holy affection they have toward God. After a few years of marriage, it is no longer biologically possible to experience the same state of sexual arousal as before. This is when boredom, both big and small, sets in, and we have already emphasized that reversing this situation is not the overcoming of boredom for Christians. Again, the Christian couple must strive together to love fervently the God who is watching over them. They must train together so that the emotions of love they express for each other flow from a holy affection toward God. Heavenly blessings will come to those couples who overcome their own stubborn hearts and work on this spiritual discipline!

Love on Another Level

As mentioned earlier, emotions, unlike affection, are physical sensations that react to a stimulus without any inclination or will. It's a kind of automatic, involuntary feeling in response to a stimulus, like how your body feels hot when the temperature rises. Sexual desire, in itself, also belongs to this category of emotions. (Technically, it's an operation of the heart that produces the emotion.) Whether you're a man or a woman, when you see an object that stimulates your sexual desire, you react to it in some way. Men are most often aroused by visual scenes, and women are most often aroused by romantic moods and kind manners.

At this point, we must recognize the nature of our emotions and train ourselves to deal with them. The emotion itself does not entail the inclination and will of our soul. That is, erotic emotions are value-neutral in themselves. Because of this quality, the character of erotic love is determined by the person to whom it is directed. When directed toward one's spouse, with whom one is covenanted before God, the emotions are beautiful and precious. But when they are directed at someone other than one's spouse, erotic emotions become ugly and impure.

The sexual desire that drives erotic emotions is also very susceptible to stimulation. It's almost an automatic reflex, whether it's physical or not. We all know from experience that when love hormones surge, we are unconsciously drawn to the person and gradually develop sexual desire toward him/her. So the way to avoid erotic emotions toward someone other than your spouse is to avoid creating those stimulating situations.

Nevertheless, certain circumstances and conditions can cause you to develop erotic emotions toward an object without realizing it. It's important to remember the *temporary attribute* of emotions. Emotions are also susceptible to familiarity, which means that if you continue to adapt to an object, you will no longer experience the same level of emotional state as before. In other words, just as erotic emotions are not as common with a spouse of many years as they were in the premarital dating, the emotions you have for someone other than your spouse are temporary and will eventually dissipate.

Therefore, we should not be overly trusting of our emotional states. While we should not blindly ignore our emotional states, we should take a firm stance against erotic emotions that are not accompanied by a holy inclination and will. You must intentionally declare to yourself that you have these emotions (or feelings). Never be deceived by the erotic emotions that sometimes arise for someone other than your spouse!

Here we see again that there must be an external force that can deal with our emotional states related to sexual desire. Because erotic emotions are vulnerable to stimulation, temporary, and almost an automatic reflex response in themselves, a holy affection that controls them is essential for Christian couples. Only when we are filled with the affection that makes us long for God through the Holy Spirit, can we fully direct our erotic emotions of love toward our spouse. This is because, as the previous diagram shows, holy affection is the covenantal framework that guards the emotion of love.

Surprisingly, the emotions of love that are formed at this time are quite different in many ways from the previous ones. First, because the emotions are captivated by the holy affection of directing them toward God, we recognize God simultaneously when we express our emotions of love toward our spouse. In other words, because the source of the emotions is God, you express your emotions of love to your spouse in a way that you love God. This means that you are overwhelmed with the awe that comes from loving God and express to your spouse emotions of love that are similar to the awe. The spouse who experiences these emotions of love feels as if God loves him/her.

Next, the emotions of love that arise from the holy affection are much more continuous and intense than those that arise from the ordinary will to love. As mentioned earlier, since the holy affection is the much more intense state of the general will to love, the emotions of love that are formed at this time are also much more intense and continuous.

Also, the emotions at this time are more continuous because

they are interlocked with the state of spiritual arousal. The emotions of love that are formed in a state of sexual arousal, even when they subside, are still filled with the holy affection that comes from a state of spiritual arousal, and so the emotions of love that are formed here continue. Therefore, they are much more continuous and intense than the emotions of love that arise from the ordinary will. Simply put, even if the sexual attraction and emotions toward your spouse are currently subdued, the Holy Spirit-filled heart that loves God will continue to manifest itself as emotions of love toward your spouse.

Finally, the emotions of love that arise from holy affection, even if they are weakened or extinguished, do not agitate us much. This is the state of marital boredom that has been properly overcome. The emotions of love that arise from the general will to love have a great impact on the "love front" of many couples, depending on the state of their emotions. So, in the beginning of a marriage, when the love hormones are high and the couple is full of love, they love each other passionately, but as the emotions of love wane over time, so does the will to love each other, and suddenly the couple becomes unstable. This is because the emotions of love that form and wane at this time are more like a state of sexual arousal.

But the emotions of love that arise from holy affection are quite different. Of course, these emotions cannot remain unchanged.

This means that the state of spiritual excitement you experience cannot be sustained, no matter how full of the Holy Spirit you are. However, because it is a state of spiritual arousal in which we are connected to God, we are not greatly disturbed by the weakening of our emotions of love, unless the holy affection is extinguished. Think of the state of fervent worship of God in a meeting, and then when the mood subsides, our souls are still fully directed toward God. Similarly, when we passionately love our spouse and the emotional state subsides, our heart is still directed toward him/her. This is because our heart is currently occupied with the holy affection that directs us toward God, who loves him/her.

In any case, Christian couples should frequently experience emotions of love that are different from those of the early years of marriage. (Herein lies the secret to overcoming marital boredom.) They should strive and train together so that the emotion of love, which was once close to a state of sexual arousal, is now captured by the holy affection that arises from a state of spiritual arousal. They should also try to experience the emotion of love that is formed from the holy affection. These two emotions of love are not an either/or proposition. They are always interlocked, though in different degrees. It is a unique dual dimension of the emotion of love that only Christian couples experience. This is because they are in a love triangle with God as the apex. In the following article, I'll show you how to share these emotions of love with each other.

1. Have you ever experienced a period of marital boredom? If so, share honestly what you did to your spouse during this time and how he/she responded. (*Note: If you are currently experiencing boredom, try to keep your emotions in check during this conversation.)

2. What do you think needs to be done to overcome marital boredom? Tell your spouse what you would like to do, not what you want him/her to do.

3. Have you ever felt different emotions of love for your spouse than you did when you were dating before marriage? If so, be specific about how it is different from premarital dating.

4. Have you ever passionately loved God and passionately desired your spouse at the same time? If so, you are experiencing the most ideal of marital communication, spiritual and sexual, at the same time. What advice would you give to couples who do not?

CHAPTER 5

A Couple Loves and Dreams Together

A Couple Dreaming of the Kingdom of God

My wife and I often talk about the kingdom of God. I don't do it out of obligation because I am a pastor, but because I sincerely long for the kingdom and we live our lives together. I often blog about my daily life, and I found a conversation I had with my wife two years ago.

> Honey, let's talk for a minute before bed. The Bible promises that the Lord is coming again. When He does, the whole world will be changed into "a new heaven and a new earth" (Rev. 21:1), and aren't you excited about life there? Paradise (the intermediate state), where our souls enter after death, is glorious, but the eternal kingdom of God that will come to earth will be even more glorious and beautiful. At the Lord's return, we will be clothed in our glorious resurrection bodies and live in that kingdom forever as the holy bride of Christ, the Bridegroom. Let's continue to live happily ever after and dream about it.

I used to say that to my wife and she'd look at me a little weirdly, but now we often have those conversations together. That is what we are married for in front of God.

Many married couples may find themselves at some point in their lives asking the question. What is the reason and purpose for staying together as a couple? We say we stay together because we love each other, but that assumes that love is constant. Unlike the people of the world, we have a noble purpose for living as a couple. It is a purpose and a reason that the world cannot imitate. In conclusion, Christian marriage is a life journey in which a loving man and woman (husband and wife) become a couple with a mission dreaming of the kingdom of God, revealing the mystical union of Christ and the church.

We can see this when we look at the first human couple. In Genesis 2, we are introduced to the first married couple. God formed Adam from the dust of the ground and put him in the garden of Eden to work it and keep it. He also gave him permission to eat of all the other fruit in the garden, except for the fruit of the tree of the knowledge of good and evil. Then God said:

> "It is not good that the man should be alone; I will make him a helper fit for him." (Gen. 2:18, ESV)

Many people misunderstand this verse. They think that God didn't like the idea of Adam living alone, so He created a helper fit for him not be lonely. This doesn't make sense given the context. Adam has no idea what it means to be lonely. Loneliness is a kind of emotional deficiency that comes from man's inability to feel God's presence, and it's a result of the fall. In Genesis 2,

Adam is still living in Eden, which is filled with God's presence before he sinned. That's why the emotion of loneliness that we feel after the fall doesn't exist for him at all.

Couples know from experience that God doesn't join people together so that they won't be lonely. When I give a lecture for couples, there's a question I often ask my audience.

"You got married because you were lonely, and now that you're together, you're not lonely anymore?"
"You got married so you wouldn't be lonely, but somehow the longer you live, the lonelier you get?"

The audience laughs at first, but then they realize that they can relate to the question. This is because they have realized that even if they married their spouse because they love him/her, they can't fully satisfy their loneliness through him/her. Of course, there is a certain amount of loneliness in a marriage. But that's only when the marriage is going well. In any case, what Genesis 2:18 says is not that it's not good for man to be lonely and alone, so God gives him a mate.

So why would God make a helper for Adam, a man living alone? The clue to why comes a few verses earlier.

The LORD God took the man and put him in the garden of Eden

to work it and keep it. (Gen. 2:15, ESV)

Adam is now the only one working and keeping the garden of Eden, where God has placed him. He's responsible for keeping the garden in good condition and for naming the animals and birds. In this context, God tells Adam that it is not good for him to be alone and that He will make a helper for him.[46]

Here we find the biblical reason for singles to meet and marry a mate. It's so that they can fulfill their God-given mission with a spouse instead of doing it alone. Specifically, God's original intention was for the wife to support the husband in his mission. We shouldn't think of a wife as inferior to her husband because she is a helper. The word for "a helper" in the Hebrew text is the noun *ezer* (עזר), which is often used to refer to God helping Israel (Deut. 33:7; Ps. 121:1, etc.).

However, since the fall, it has become a reality that the original roles of husband and wife before the fall cannot be fulfilled, which means that the roles of the couple are sometimes reversed. It is possible for a husband to play a supporting role in his wife's mission. Therefore, it is not necessary to focus on the mission of either the husband or the wife. Rather, it should be seen as a part-

★

46) In verses 20-22, we see Adam naming the animals on his own, and it's in this context that God gives him a helper.

nership in mission between the husband and wife.

And Adam's situation is actually a mirror image of ours today. Adam was placed in Eden by God and given the mission of working and keeping it. Eden at this time was sinless and full of God's presence, foreshadowing the perfect kingdom of God that will come to us in the future. In other words, the garden of Eden in the beginning is a prototype of the kingdom of God. In terms of God's rule, we live in His kingdom that has already come. It has been in full swing since the resurrection of Christ.[47] This is so because the resurrection that will take place on the day when the kingdom of God comes has already taken place in Christ.

So we live in the kingdom of God that has already come and hope for the kingdom of God that is to come. The same God who led Adam into Eden has now led us, the Christians, into the kingdom of God that has already come. The God who gave Adam the mission of working and keeping Eden has now given us the mission of "working and keeping" the kingdom of God that has already come. However, the kingdom of God that has already come in which we live is the "garden of Eden" that has lost its original appearance. The mission of working and keeping it is all of our actions that contribute to restoring Eden to its original state or bet-

★

47) For a general overview of the concept of the kingdom of God, see *A Theology of Dating*, 35–38.

ter. God can do it without us, but He wants to use our half-hearted obedience, prayers, and devotion.

This is the existential situation in which we all find ourselves in. It is the Lord's longing that the sin-stained kingdom of God be "worked" and restored to its original beauty through us, who have first experienced the gospel of the cross. Genesis 2:18 applies to us today when it says that God does not like the idea of man doing this work alone.

I realized this even before I got married, and I wanted to dedicate my life to working and keeping Eden with my wife, and I still talk to her a lot about the kingdom of God, and we are both passionate about the mission God has given us. Of course, at one point, my passion for the mission got the best of me and I became a workaholic. But now, even though my life is busier than it was then, my love for my wife is growing deeper and deeper. I love my wife more and more because I am so happy to live with her, dreaming of the kingdom of God and fulfilling the mission God has given us as a couple. So the emotions of love I share with my wife these days are different than before. It's not a dynamic emotional state, but it feels like another level of romance where we deeply long for each other. As I argued earlier, it is a love that comes from a holy affection.

🔔 A Couple on a Mission Armed with Love

Christian marriage is a journey that a "loving" couple on a mission dream of the kingdom of God. It's not just a couple that dreams of the kingdom of God and only fulfills their mission. Christian marriage is composed of two pillars: love and mission. A marriage without love is prone to compulsive workaholism, and a marriage without mission is like a ship at sea without direction. Twelve years ago, my marriage was more like the former.

The Korean church has traditionally favored marriages with a mission than love. Especially ministerial couples have willingly or unwillingly brainwashed themselves into thinking that such marriages are biblical and ideal. They have been so devoted to the church that they have neglected their own families, the smallest unit of the church. It is no exaggeration to say that the revival of the Korean church, which is rare in the history of the church, was built on the sacrifice of families. I was often advised by senior pastors to stay away from my wife and children in church and avoid looking at them.

On the other hand, there seem to be a lot of "missionless" marriages in the Korean church these days. It seems that members have a strong sense that their family is everything in their lives rather than a sense of mission to build the kingdom of God together through the church. Older generations still have a sense of community and will sometimes leave their families behind and give their possessions and time for the sake of the church and the kingdom of God. But younger generations are more and more willing to make commitments only in areas related to personal and family interests rather than to the church. Pastors are no exception. They seem to love their families too much rather than the church. They should be guaranteed the right to go home as soon as it is time to leave the church, even if their work is not finished. There are some pastors who have a family emergency in their community, and when the senior pastor calls the pastor late at night to invite him to come, he is proud to say that he can go tomorrow. This is because he has to "love" his own families more.

In any case, married couples must balance both love and mission. It's not an either/or proposition. Let's take a look at how love and mission should be harmonized in the Bible text.

Let's go back to Genesis 2, where we started. God planted the garden of Eden, formed Adam from the dust of the ground, and gave him the mission of working and keeping it. Then one day God caused a deep sleep to fall on Adam, took one of his ribs, formed a woman from it, and brought her to him. When Adam saw her, he fell in love with her and sang a beautiful wedding song: "This at last is bone of my bones and flesh of my flesh" (2:23). This was the first love affair of mankind, and the first marriage.

In this way, it can be understood that God's mission to Adam came first, and love came after. This logic makes sense, except for God. However, as we argue in this book, Christian marriage is a covenantal triangle with God as the apex. Everyone first enters into a covenant relationship with God before they meet their mate. In other words, when we are united to Christ in the Holy Spirit, we form a vertical covenant relationship with God. Simply put, we first experience a spiritual marriage relationship with Christ as the Bridegroom by making love to Him. It is in this state that we meet our mate, make love to him/her, and get married.

The same is true of Adam in Genesis 2. He first experienced a covenant relationship with God before he was given a mission by God.[48] His existence came into being when God formed him from the dust of the ground and breathed into his nostrils the breath of life — or, to put it more romantically, God expressing His love to Adam. It's like a man and woman in love, face to face, sharing the breath of love. If the creation of the heavens and the earth was an overflowing of the love (because of the overflowing nature of love) that the Triune God shared from eternity, then when God created Adam, His love overflowed and enveloped his being.

So Adam came into the world with God's love. One day, God

★

48) The Westminster Standards say that God made a covenant of works (or covenant of life) with Adam (see WCF, Ch 7.2; WLC, Q 20; WSC, Q 12).

gave him a mission to work and keep Eden. This means to fulfill his mission with a heart that loves God and in a way that over-flows outwardly. In this state, God sent Adam a helper, Eve. When Adam saw her, he sang a "wedding song" and fell in love, and the couple's love began. At this point, their love must have been a tremendous driving force in fulfilling the mission God had given them, not just for its own sake.

To summarize, Adam, having formed a loving relationship with God, was given a mission by God and was responding faith-fully to that mission, and then he met the woman God sent to him and began another loving relationship, and their love fueled them to fulfill the mission God had given them. To summarize in one line.

Love (with God) → Mission (from God) → Love (with spouse) → Mission (with spouse)

As you can see, when it comes down to "love first or mis-sion first," love comes first. A loving relationship with God is the foundation of all missionary endeavors, and it also holds fast to a loving relationship with a spouse. This fact means that if our rela-tionship with God is broken, our mission is broken, and our rela-tionship with our spouse is broken. Therefore, anyone who wants to live as a person with a mission must first arm themselves with the love of God. God's love is a tremendous power that transforms a sinner into a righteous person and enables him/her to live a new life. When you are captivated by this love, you cannot stand still! The attribute of love overflows outward, so the renewed person wants to express his/her love for God in some way. At this point, God entrusts him/her with a noble mission. God lets him/her go through life expressing his/her love for God to the fullest.

To such a person, God sends a "helper." It is better to fulfill the mission together in passionate love than to fulfill it alone. This is the same way the Triune God loves one another completely and works together in everything He does. Because God created us in His image, He wants us to live our lives in His likeness.

If you are a Christian couple reading this, I invite you to consider. Are you dreaming of the kingdom of God? Do you live your lives on a mission to help bring it about? How often do you have conversations with your spouse about this mission? How much does the energy of love that flows between you affect how you fulfill that mission?

If you can't answer any of these questions, you need to redefine the purpose and reason for your marriage. Christian marriage should be radically different from the world! In the world, their primary purpose is to find the love of their life and to keep that love alive in marriage. But we have a clear purpose and reason for marriage. It is to fulfill a God-given mission together as a couple in hope of the kingdom to come. This is not an easy task, so we must first be filled with the love of God and armed with love for each other. Then we can use the energy of that love to comfort and encourage each other and fulfill the mission. Can we say that our marriage is in such a state now?

What Is a Couple's Mission Together?

At this point, a question may arise. Now that we know that Christian marriages are meant to dream of the kingdom of God as a couple with a mission, armed with love, the following question may arise: What is the mission that a couple fulfills together? In the garden of Eden, the mission given to Adam and Eve was to work and to keep it. Since Eden is said to be a prototype of the kingdom of God, we can say that the mission of Christian couples today is to work and to keep the kingdom of God. What does that mean for us?

First of all, the words *work* and *keep* (Gen. 2:15) have a lot to do with the *cultural mandate* that God gave to human beings.[49] That is to say, God didn't create humans to be just a part of nature, but rather to rule over and care for creation. To *work* (or to *culti-*

---

49) 신국원, 『신국원의 문화 이야기』 (서울: 한국기독학생회출판부, 2002), 136.

vate) means that humans are to actively utilize nature and develop it through creative activity, and to *keep* means that we are to act as stewards (or caretakers) of God's creation, caring for and protecting it. So when we say that we are to work and keep the kingdom of God, it means that we are to develop it through creative activity and to care for and protect it to ensure its continuation.

Ever since sin entered the world, there has been a break in God's kingdom. It was divided into two realms: the realm where God's rule still reigns and the realm where sin is allowed under God's sovereignty. Christian couples live a life ruled by God because they believe in the gospel, and they long for Eden, which God created beautifully in the beginning, and hope that the perfect state of Eden will come to this earth. This is the context in which we live our lives.

So how do we apply the idea of working and keeping the kingdom of God to us? We can think of all the ways in which we advance, maintain, and care for the kingdom of God (all the realms over which God reigns) in our daily lives in this sinful world. On a public level, this is often seen in relation to our job, and on a private level, it is all aspects of our daily lives.

How can we fulfill mission in the realm of our job? I serve as a chaplain in a hospital, so I'll start with healthcare workers. Healthcare workers fulfill the kingdom of God by saving and sustaining life. The kingdom of God to come is a place where there is no death, no pain, and no sickness. Paradise, where our *souls* enter after death, is such a place, but the eternal kingdom of God that we so look forward to is the perfect one that will begin on earth at the Lord's return. When the time comes, our souls and bodies will be reunited and we will be transformed into glorified resurrection bodies.[50] In other words, we will be in perfect health and will never die. Therefore, the medical work of healthcare workers has a special significance in that it does not merely cure disease, but contributes to the restoration of perfect health that will take place in His kingdom in the sight of God. Of course, the medical work itself does not bring about perfect health at that time. The Lord Himself will provide that perfect state on that day. Until then, however, the work of God's kingdom (healing and restoration) is partially experienced through their medical works.

The same is true in any other workplace. We should give meaning to our work and take pride in how it contributes to the kingdom of God. A florist shows people the beauty of the kingdom of God, a lawyer works to bring God's justice and righteousness to the earth, and so on. Aside from the people of the world, we Christians should be constantly thinking about how all of our work can contribute to the kingdom of God, no matter what job we are in.

★
50) See the answer to Q. 87 in the Westminster Shorter Catechism.

The same is true of those who struggle to make a living. Of course, we should not make light of their difficulties, but they should have hope that the very place they are in will be transformed into the kingdom of God in the future. When the Lord returns, every place on earth will be transformed into the perfect kingdom of God. That is why we Christians should live dreaming of the kingdom of God with all our might, even at work. No matter how much we suffer injustice, we will be heirs of the world on the last day (Rom. 4:13). We should truly believe that the Lord will come again and transform the whole world into a perfect state, which will be inherited by all of us! If these words sound unfamiliar and awkward, I encourage you to read the Bible again.

So we were called to be a great couple with a mission. We live our lives as a beautiful, loving couple, dreaming of the kingdom of God. When a husband or wife comes home from a hard day's work, how should they comfort each other? In addition to human comfort, shouldn't they renew their spiritual commitment by dreaming together of the eternal kingdom together? Shouldn't they share the hardships of the workplace, protest the injustices of the world, and ultimately set their hope on the day when the Lord returns to this world?

Of course, there is a good chance that our physical life will end before then and our souls will go to *Paradise* first. Nevertheless, we must remember that it is not our final destination. Those who think that the place where our souls enter after death is the last place are not very much in love with this earth. Not in a good way, but in the sense that they have little holy desire to live passionately and according to the Word here on earth. Why is this? Because they think that when they die, leaving this sinful and troubled world is their final salvation.

But this is not true! God does not give up on this world. He will definitely restore it to the original (or even better) beautiful and glorious Eden that He created. When He returns, He will settle this sinful, troubled world once and for all. On that day, all sin and injustice will be gone, all ecosystems will be fully restored, and there will be no more death, suffering, or disease. This is what the Bible calls our final salvation.

Christian couples, as well as all Christians, live for that very day. So we are all given a mission for the kingdom of God in every area of our lives. We are all given a mission on a personal level in our daily lives. Christian couples should show their children the relationship between Christ and the church through their love and happiness with each other. This is where home education begins. Children realize God's love and grace as they are loved by their parents. Outside of the home and the church, they should be able to live as if the kingdom of heaven had come to earth. Of course, we must recognize that this is not easy because of the sinfulness and unrighteousness of the world. That's why we need to pray with tears and ask for the rule of God to come not only in the homes and churches, but in every part of the world. Shouldn't Christian couples in particular live this beautiful life?

Christian couples must be clear and organized about what their current mission is. I'm not saying to get a new job. Mission is not synonymous with a job (or workplace). A job is just a means to a mission. God is not that interested in what kind of job we have. He's much more interested in what we do with it and how we live it out. This is our mission. Because when the Lord returns, it will be transformed into the kingdom of God. He wants us to live out the kingdom of God as best we can in our workplaces and in our homes before He returns.

You can change jobs throughout your life. It's safe to say that the concept of a lifetime job is dead. Wherever we find ourselves, our mission is to use our workplace as a means to serve our co-workers and our company with the principles of the gospel. The shape and manner in which we fulfill this mission varies from person to person. A married couple can have different jobs and still fulfill their mission. You can fulfill your mission for the kingdom of God by communicating together in a way that is beneficial to your faith and family life. When we think of the garden of Eden in the beginning, don't we want to dream of a beautiful and perfect world with our spouse?

Precious Because You Are Not Permanent

I once read John Piper's *This Momentary Marriage: A Parable of Permanence*. From the title, we can see at a glance what characterizes Christian marriage: that our marriage is temporary, not permanent. This is a statement with which everyone agrees, since couples cannot live together forever without dying. But we say *temporary* not simply because we can't stay together forever, but because we serve as a shadow of what is eternal. This is illustrated by Jesus' words in the *Resurrection Debate* in Matthew 22. The Sadducees, who don't believe in the resurrection, come to Jesus and ask Him questions with the intention of tricking him.

> 24 saying: "Teacher, Moses said that if a man dies, having no children, his brother shall marry his wife and raise up offspring for his brother. 25 Now there were with us seven brothers. The first died after he had married, and having no offspring, left his wife to his brother. 26 Likewise the second also, and the third, even to the seventh. 27 Last of all the woman died also. 28 Therefore, in the resurrection, whose wife of the seven will she be? For they all had her." (Matt. 22:24-28)

The point they are trying to make is that if there is a resurrection, there may be serious complications in marital relationships

when a person is widowed and remarries. According to the Mosaic Law, when an older brother dies, the younger brother must
marry the older brother's wife to continue the line, and if seven
brothers each marry a woman in this way, whose wife will she be
in the resurrection? So, if there is a resurrection, there is a serious
situation of seven men with one woman and the problem of their
wives.

Then Jesus answered, "You are mistaken, not knowing the
Scriptures nor the power of God" (22:29), and said a significant
word.

> For in the resurrection they neither marry nor are given in mar-
> riage, but are like angels of God in heaven. (Matt. 22:30)

He is saying that in the resurrection, people will neither marry
nor be given in marriage; in other words, there will be no more
marriages. The Sadducees thought that if there is a resurrection,
the current system of marriage will continue after the resurrection,
but Jesus' words directly deny their idea. The resurrection will be
a completely different world than the one we live in now, so there
will be no need for the current institution of marriage to exist.

This is because the temporal institution of marriage is a temporary shadow of what is eternal. The Bible frequently compares our
relationship with God to that of a husband and wife. Of course,

there are other analogies, such as a father's relationship with his children, a king's relationship with his people, and so on. But we should pay special attention to the analogy of a husband and wife (or a bride and groom). His unbreakable love, the love that unites two different beings into one, the love that refuses to give up no matter what, is most vividly revealed through the man and woman in marriage.

The relationship between Christ the Bridegroom and His holy bride, the Church, is one of permanence! It is a covenant relationship of love that began on earth but continues forever. The earthly, momentary analogy of this eternal thing is the institution of marriage. Therefore, while the love of a married couple is indeed precious and noble, it is not eternal. Even the most loving couple must remember that they are on a journey through life together, looking toward the eternal. As you grow older, you will realize that one day you will have to leave the one you love and go to your eternal Bridegroom. Perhaps you are enjoying a temporary marriage here on earth in order to properly love your eternal Bridegroom in the eternal kingdom of God.

It's important to remember that a couple's love won't last forever, which makes them even more precious to each other. When passengers are on an airplane that crashes due to a terrorist attack or accident and realize that they're about to die, there's a common reaction. Every single one of them, without exception, leaves a message to their families saying that they are sorry and that they love them. Why do they do this? Because the few remaining minutes and seconds trigger feelings of not loving them more and make them regret their shortcomings, so they want to tell them that they love them, even if it's just for a few last moments.

We must remember that the relationship between a husband and wife is in the same situation. In the context of eternity, the time a couple has together is a fleeting moment. The title of John Piper's book, *This Momentary Marriage*, is actually close to that. The word *momentary* is more often used to mean *fleeting* than *temporary*. It's a marriage of this fleeting moment that represents something eternal. We can feel the author's longing for something eternal in marriage. In any case, we should always keep in mind that our love with our spouse is not eternal and that he/she is precious. What is your current state of heart toward him/her? Do you want to react like a passenger on an airplane that is about to leave the world?

The Mystical Union of Christ and the Church

Now we come to perhaps the most important aspect of Christian marriage. Let me repeat the concluding statement I mentioned earlier. Christian marriage is a life journey that reveals the mystical union of Christ and the church, in which a loving man and woman (husband and wife) become a couple with a mission, dreaming of the kingdom of God. The Christian couple, armed with love, fulfills a mission for the kingdom of God, and their very life together is a reflection of Christ and the church to their neighbors.

God has joined us together as couples with a mission for a noble purpose. It is to share love and mission together, and ultimately to witness to the world about Christ and the church. To put it in terms, Christian marriage is directly related to ecclesiology (i.e., the study of the church) and, by extension, to missiology. Since a married couple or family (including children) is the smallest unit of the church, the church is healthy when their marriage is happy in Christ, and it can have a good influence on neighbors when the church is healthy and happy in the Holy Spirit. This is evangelism and mission in relation to marriage.

As I've mentioned several times, Paul referred to Christian marriage as "a great mystery" and said that he spoke "concerning Christ and the church" (Eph. 5:31-32). He was moved by the Holy Spirit as he read Genesis 2:24[51] and realized that the verse ultimately foreshadowed the mystical union of Christ and the church.

★

51) Therefore a man shall leave his father and mother and be joined to his wife, and they shall become one flesh.

For the Holy Spirit revealed such a mystery to Paul because it meant that when God created the institution of marriage in Eden, He already had in mind what Christ and the church would look like in the distant future.

Such a great vision of God should always be on the minds of Christian couples. In this article, rather than theologizing about the mystical union of Christ and the church, we will examine our marriages through real-life examples. In *A Theology of Dating*, I introduced the story of Mr. and Mrs. Nick Vujicic. His story of falling in love and marrying a woman with no limbs has touched many. Their burning love, despite their outward appearance, seems to us like a mystical union between Christ and the church.

There are couples in the Korean church who share such love. I don't dare to introduce my story because of my failures until 12 years ago, but I would like to introduce the story of a pastor I know. It is the marriage story of a pastor who ministers to the visually impaired. As a young man, he was introduced to the blind community and was called to become a pastor and live for the blind. When he was full of grace, he even prayed like this.

God, how do you want to use me? I know the blind well, but I can't understand their hearts. So I would rather be blind and pastor them, and if I am blind, will they turn to God? If that happens, I don't mind being blind. Please make me blind.[52]

It is an odd and amazing prayer. But no matter how many times he prayed, he never got an answer. So one day, on the advice of a blind church brother, he changed his prayer. The pastor's eyes must be able to see well in order to minister to the blind. So he changed his prayer to this.

> God, please let me find a blind spouse with whom I can pastor for the rest of my life rather than becoming blind myself. Let me find a spouse with whom I can share the same faith, comfort each other, and have a good heart, so that God's glory will be shown when we evangelize the blind. The blind will see us and know that it is not difficult to marry and live well with the able-bodied. And the able-bodied will see and know that it is not difficult to marry and live well with the blind![53]

One day, he met the woman he was meant to meet. She was thirteen years his senior and the leader of a Christian fellowship for the blind. They realized they had a mutual attraction, and after persistent courtship and persuasion, she agreed to marry him. The problem was the disapproval of her family. They couldn't understand why a bachelor with all his limbs would want to marry

★

52) 정민교, 『빛 가운데로 걸어가면』 (서울: 세움북스, 2023), 199. I translated the Korean paragraph into English.

53) Ibid., 200-201.

their daughter. Her parents insisted on seeing his family register or a certificate of family relationship, just in case he had failed to marry before or had children he was hiding. Nevertheless, he endured all the difficulties and finally succeeded in marrying a blind woman 13 years his senior. His prayers were answered within five years.

I heard this couple's story in person with my wife. As I listened to their marriage story, someone kept coming to my mind. The image of Jesus, our eternal Bridegroom, was playing in my mind. How could He, who had the best qualifications in the universe, leave nothing to be desired and come to earth as a Man, chase after spiritually handicapped sinners, claiming to love them, and then die on a cross to prove His love for us as His bride? This is a love that is incomprehensible by human standards. It is a mystical union between Jesus and His body, the Church. He wants this union to be witnessed to the whole world through Christian couples.

Another story I'd like to share is from the family of a patient who was admitted to the hospital where I serve as a chaplain.[54] One day in August 2020, I received an urgent call from the surgeon saying that a dying patient wanted a bedside baptism. I walked into the room, ready to send a soul to Paradise, and the dying woman was trembling and sobbing, asking to be baptized. I asked her to confirm her confession of faith, to see if she could answer.

Do you believe that the Lord Jesus Christ is the Son of God and the Savior of sinners, and that He is your only hope in all circumstances?

Near the end of her life, she had little energy to answer, so her family joined with her to strengthen her frail voice. As a chaplain, I was convinced of the birth of new life and performed a bedside baptism on the patient.

Mrs. Mary, who believes in the Lord Jesus, I baptize you in the name of the Father, and of the Son, and of the Holy Spirit.

The woman standing next to me took a moment to share her story of struggle. She told me that she had married her blind husband and lived her life by faith alone. She said that she had been praying all her life for her mother's salvation, and she was so happy that her prayers had finally been answered.

It was then that I was able to witness the mystical union of Christ and the church. His coming as a light to God's people in spiritual darkness was being witnessed in this woman's life. The story of this woman's marriage is a cautionary tale for many couples who marry on all sorts of terms and then divorce because their hearts are not in it. Years later, I was preaching at a church and the couple was sitting there. They came over to say hello after the service, and I still remember how beautiful they looked.

🔔 First Love and Last Love

Generally, men tend to reminisce about their first love more often than women. This means that men and women have different attitudes toward love. There are many reasons why men are more likely to talk about their first love. But it's probably because they experienced their first love during adolescence, when sex hormones increase rapidly, and the memory of it remains intense. Whether it was unrequited love or mutual love, the memory of that time remains the purest for men.

Women, on the other hand, don't talk much about their first love. There are many possible explanations for this, but one of them is that women are much more used to emotional love than men. So when they "really" break up and meet another man, they completely erase the feelings of love that they shared with their ex-boyfriend. Therefore, when they meet and fall in love with another man, the memories and feelings are already gone. Of course, they will still have the memories, but they won't affect their relationship with their current lover.

Perhaps because of these masculine and feminine traits, the Irish playwright Oscar Wilde (1854-1900) wrote a wonderful line about love.

Men always want to be a woman's first love - women like to be a man's last romance.[55]

Men want to remain that way for women because of their intense memories of their first love, and women want to remain that way for their current man because they want to erase their previous man from their memory. How, then, should we understand the nature of love, and should we simply categorize it as "first love for men and last love for women" according to the inclinations of men and women? In keeping with the title of this book, *A Theology for Married Couples*, let's take a biblical and covenantal look at the attribute of love.

In *A Theology of Dating*, I said that we should correct the concept of first love. Generally speaking, first love refers to the first person you fall in love with. In other words, it is the first love

★

55) Oscar Wilde online, "A Woman of No Importance," accessed December 17, 2024, https://www.wilde-online.info/a-woman-of-no-importance-page12.html.

experienced chronologically. But that's not what we say when we understand the nature of love. We should establish how we conceptualize first love based on the Bible and organize our thinking around it. This is a topic I covered in *A Theology of Dating*, but I want to highlight it in more detail in the context of marriage. Interestingly, there is a text in the Bible that uses the phrase *first love*. It is Revelation 2:4[56], but let's take a look at different translations.

> Nevertheless I have *this* against you, that you have left your first love. (NKJV)
>
> Yet I hold this against you: You have forsaken the love you had at first. (NIV)

This verse is a warning from the Lord to the church in Ephesus. The preceding context describes how much they had labored and persevered for the Lord. Nevertheless, they were rebuked by the Lord because they had forsaken their "first love." This means that they had lost the initial passion and love they had for the Lord. Interestingly, the passion was still there. But it's just that it did't come from a heart that loved the Lord. No matter how much they labored and had a zeal for the Lord, if they were not moti-

★

56) The Greek text also says "your first love" (τὴν ἀγάπην σου πρώτην).

vated by that initial love, their labor and zeal became a legalistic compulsion and were of little value to the Lord.

This applies equally to a couple's marriage. Usually, when a couple is newly married, they really love each other and act passionately toward each other. If the wife is sick, the husband will take care of her with genuine concern, and if the husband is having a hard time at work, the wife will comfort him and cook him a hot meal. (The roles can just as easily be reversed.) In addition to these everyday things, on their anniversary or birthday, they will organize a surprise event to surprise their husband or wife. This is because the love they had at the beginning is still there, and whatever they do is motivated by love.

But over time, there is an inner change. There is not much outward change. When the wife's health deteriorates, the husband takes care of her as best he can, and when the husband comes home tired from work, the wife fulfills her role as usual. When the calendar reminds him of an upcoming birthday or anniversary, he still buys and delivers a gift to her. But something is missing. The couple gradually realizes that they don't have the love they had at the beginning. Wives are much more sensitive to this than husbands, so they often complain to their husbands that they don't want gifts, they want his heart. She wants to reaffirm the love they shared at the beginning. This is similar to the state of the Ephesian church in Revelation 2. In that context, first love refers to "the love you had at first," as the NIV Bible translates it.

Now let's look at another aspect of first love. Primarily, the phrase *first love* in Revelation 2:4 refers to the love they first had for the Lord immediately after their conversion.[57] It's worth noting the phrase "immediately after their conversion." Conversion is our response to the new birth (regeneration) wrought by the Holy Spirit, which consists of the elements of faith and repentance. Conversion, then, is interlocked with the beginning of our covenant relationship with Christ. In other words, the spiritual marriage relationship began when Christ, the Bridegroom, accepted us as His bride. The love that begins for us at this time is also called the *first love*. This love is based on the covenant that He made with us. So when we talk about first love, we should remember that it has more to do with an irrevocable covenant than with a chronological sense.

Consider this. We often sing the worship song "Jesus, You Alone Shall Be My First Love" by Tim Hughes. But is Jesus really our first love in a chronological sense? What were we in love with in the past before we accepted Jesus as our Bridegroom? Were we not unknowingly in a perverse love affair with "the prince of the power of the air" (Eph. 2:2), living a life away from God? Then, by the work of the Holy Spirit, we received Jesus and

★

57) Grant R. Osborne, *Revelation*, BECNT (Grand Rapids, MI: Baker Academic, 2002), 115.

now we sing "very brazenly" that He is our first love. But God is pleased to accept this brazen confession because the meaning of first love is based on the covenant between Him and us. Although He is not the first in chronological order, He accepts our hearts toward Him as "first love" because of the covenant of love, which is irrevocable and unbreakable.

Also, this first love now becomes the last love because under no circumstances can we leave our Bridegroom and because no matter what happens, our eternal Bridegroom will not abandon us. The love we share with Him becomes the *last first love*. In the context of love, we are first and last with Him forever.

Now let's turn our attention to horizontal covenant relationships. We've all been in love with someone before we met our spouse. We usually refer to that first experience of love as our first love. However, this was before marriage and not a covenant relationship. It's just a romantic relationship with the possibility of breaking up. Then one day you break up, fall in love with someone else, and finally marry that person. You have entered into a covenant relationship, a lifelong commitment.

So think about who your first love is. Think about who that first love is that you should base your covenant on. Your spouse, the person with whom you now share your life, is your *first love*! If you still don't understand what I mean, read the previous paragraph again. Remember that the meaning of "first" should be based on the marriage covenant. You shouldn't be stuck with a chronological first love anymore. So, even if it seems very shameless, you should often confess to your husband or wife, "You are my first love!"

Furthermore, we should say, "You are my last love," because covenant-based love cannot be broken. Remembering that the eternal Bridegroom is our first and last love, we should take to heart that this principle should apply to our spouse as well. So every Christian couple actually spends their lives with their *last first love*. Although Oscar Wilde said that a man wants to be a woman's first love and a woman likes to be a man's last love, Christian couples should say to each other that they will spend their lives with both their first and last love. Heavenly blessings be upon couples who make this confession of love often!

1. How often do you and your spouse talk about the kingdom of God? Or have you never had a conversation about it?

2. Are you convinced that you and your spouse are called to be a couple with a mission for the kingdom of God? If so, what is your mindset and attitude at home and at work?

3. How are you working specifically to demonstrate the relationship between Christ and the church through your marriage?

4. Do you believe that you share a covenant-based *first love* with your spouse since the time of your marriage? Share with each other again what the concept of first and last love means to you.

CHAPTER 6

Enjoy a Happy Marriage

Marital Sex to Renew the Covenant

Christian couples who confess their spouse as their *first love* have an obligation to maintain and renew that love. A couple's love is to be affirmed in all aspects of their lives, but especially in their marital sex. The Bible actively authorizes sexual activity within the covenantal framework of marriage (Gen. 2:24; Lev. 20:10; 1 Cor. 7:3-5, etc.). Marital sex is more than just a means of satisfying desires. There are many different meanings that can be drawn from this, but let's focus on the covenantal aspect.

As we have emphasized many times, the vertical and horizontal covenants are intertwined in every way. In other words, the elements that characterize the relationship between God and us in terms of covenant also apply to the relationship between a husband and wife. In the Holy Spirit, we are united with Christ and enter into a covenant of love with God. This covenant, once made, is never broken and continues forever. The place where we recognize that this covenant continues is in Sunday worship. That is why it has been said that worship is "the scene of covenant renewal."[58] Through worship, we experience God's covenantal love again and live our daily lives in the power of that love. When the grace of the Holy Spirit is poured out in fullness through the

★

58) 권기현, 『예배 중에 찾아오시는 우리 하나님』 (경산: 도서출판 R&F, 2019), 23-24.

proclaimed Word, every part of our soul is exposed to the Triune God as it is, willing and eager to be ruled by Him.

This is also true for couples who are in a horizontal covenant. There are many elements, but the marital sex is the most important one. Their *first love* began when the bride and groom made their marriage vows before God and the officiant guaranteed their vows in the name of the Triune God. The bride and groom first affirm their covenantal love on the first night through passionate kissing and sexual intercourse. It is a sublime moment when their marriage covenant is affirmed through the sexual act, exposing themselves completely to him/her and willingly allowing their will and emotions to be controlled by him/her.

This beautiful and sublime moment doesn't happen just once. Each couple is different, but depending on their age and circumstances, their marital sex is cyclical. Since their marital sex began with the affirmation of the covenant made on their wedding day, the marital sex that follows is very much a renewal of the marriage covenant.[59] It's more than just a way to satisfy a desire. Therefore, Christian couples should approach sex in a fundamentally different way than the people of the world. We should rejoice in the fact that we are being faithful to our marriage covenant, reaffirming our oneness as one flesh, even if we sometimes do not

★

59) 팀 켈러, 『팀 켈러, 결혼을 말하다』, 최종훈 옮김 (서울: 두란노, 2014), 294-301.

experience as much sexual pleasure or orgasm as before.

So what is the current state of your marital sex with your spouse? Do you view marital sex as a way to renew your marriage covenant, or do you simply want your spouse to be more intentional about satisfying your desires? Are you willing to allow your body and heart to be controlled by your spouse during marital sex, or do you want to control and dominate your spouse's body? Remember that your current sexual attitude toward your spouse is directly related to your attitude toward God. As emphasized earlier, especially for married couples, there is no fundamental difference between how you treat God and how you treat your spouse.

Kissing, a Sublime Act of Homage

In *A Theology of Dating*, I advised unmarried couples not to engage in the act of kissing. I'm not talking about a gentle kiss on the lips as a greeting, but a *deep kiss* with sexual connotations. That is, the exchange of tongues is an attempt to bring each other's desires to a climax that leads directly to intercourse.

Kissing of this nature is only permitted between married couples because of the covenantal nature of kissing. The Bible only allows sexual activity for married couples, and it doesn't just refer to sexual intercourse. It includes all sexual behaviors (genital stimulation, deep kissing, etc.) that move toward the climax of sexual activity, which is intercourse. In particular, the act of kissing is almost equated with the marital sex. In *A Theology of Dating*, I touched briefly on kissing in relation to the permissible level of physical contact, but now I will discuss it in more detail in relation to the marital sex.

If you search the Bible for the word *kiss*, you'll find a total of 48 occurrences.[60] While most of these refer to a traditional greeting from the ancient Near East, there are also passages that refer to the act of kissing in a sexual sense.[61] Most notably, it's explicitly introduced in the Song of Solomon, a beautifully written song about a marital passion.

> Let him kiss me with the kisses of his mouth—for your love is more delightful than wine. (Song 1:2, NIV)

In this verse, the Shulammite wants King Solomon to kiss her deeply. This would not be out of place for a couple to express to each other today. The kiss in this verse is not just a greeting, but a sexual act shared by a loving couple. What's more, it's not an act

★

60) This is the result of a search in the Logos Bible using English Bibles such as the NKJV, ESV, and NIV. A search for the Hebrew word (נשק) yields 32 occurrences in the Old Testament, two of which are translated differently (Gen. 41:40; Ezek. 3:13).

61) Job 31:27; Prov. 7:13; Amos 1:2; 8:1.

that comes from a mere sexual impulse, but a romantic kiss that comes "out of sincere love and respect for the person."[62] In any case, the meaning is that the act of kissing in a sexual sense must be accompanied by sincere love and respect for the person.

Interestingly, the word *kiss* also has religious and spiritual connotations.[63] In the Old Testament, *kiss* is used to refer to the act of worshiping an idol such as Baal (1 Kings 19:18). The act of kissing implies that you have a special relationship with the idol. It is an act of homage, submission, and loyalty to that idol,[64] and it signifies that you will no longer serve any other gods, but only Baal, which is called *covenantal loyalty*. In this context, the word *kiss* is also used for God.

Kiss the Son, lest He be angry, And you perish *in* the way, When His wrath is kindled but a little. Blessed *are* all those who put their trust in Him. (Ps. 2:12)

"The Son" here refers to "My Son" in verse 7,[65] the Mes-

★

62) 강병도 편, 『카리스 종합주석 제51권: 전도서, 아가』 (서울: 기독지혜사, 2014), 540.

63) 1 Kings 19:18; Psalm 2:12; 85:10; Hos. 13:2.

64) Victor Harold Matthews et al, *The IVP Bible Background Commentary: Old Testament*, electronic ed. (Downers Grove, IL: InterVarsity Press, 2000), 1 Kings 19:18.

65) "I will declare the decree: The LORD has said to Me, 'You are My Son, Today I have begotten You.

siah (Christ) whom God would send. So when we are told to *kiss* God's Son, it means to show the highest homage, submission, and loyalty to His Son, Christ.[66] It is to give covenantal loyalty to the Son and to no other idol. Thus, the word *kiss* presupposes a special relationship between the parties that cannot be interrupted by a third party. It indicates a covenant relationship.

As mentioned earlier, the elements that characterize the relationship between God and us in terms of covenant also apply to the relationship between a husband and wife. So the meaning of *kiss* can be applied correspondingly. The act of kissing (deep kissing), then, is reserved for couples in a covenant relationship. It's a noble act of homage, submission, and loyalty to one's spouse. So you shouldn't be impatient to satisfy your own needs first. You should prioritize your spouse's feelings and emotional state, and maintain the attitude that you want to satisfy him/her well. The act of kissing should not be based on sexual urges alone, but on sincere love and respect for the person. In this beautiful and sublime atmosphere, the husband and wife embark on a passionate journey toward marital love, the peak of sexual activity. In this context, the act of kissing is the final gateway to climax and can never be separated from marital sex.

★

66) So the NASB English Bible translates it as "Do homage to the Son."

✒ The Joy of Satisfying Your Spouse

Husbands and wives are meant to bring sexual pleasure and satisfaction to each other. If they are ascetic and refuse to have sex, or if they are hedonistic and are only concerned with satisfying their own sexual desires, both are contrary to what the Bible says about sex. The apostle Paul addressed the Corinthian church on the issue of marriage, and his message is as relevant today as it was then, providing crucial guidance on marital sex.

> 3 Let the husband render to his wife the affection due her, and likewise also the wife to her husband. 4 The wife does not have authority over her own body, but the husband *does*. And likewise the husband does not have authority over his own body, but the wife *does*. 5 Do not deprive one another except with consent for a time, that you may give yourselves to fasting and prayer; and come together again so that Satan does not tempt you because of your lack of self-control. (1 Cor. 7:3-5)

For one thing, Paul's teaching was truly shocking given the first-century climate that treated women as the property of their husbands. "The wife does not have authority over her own body, but the husband *does*" would have sounded obvious to men in Paul's day, but "likewise the husband does not have authority over his own body, but the wife *does*" would have been completely out of the question. Furthermore, the idea of temporarily abstaining from marital sex, "except with consent for a time" would have sounded radical to his readers.[67] In the first-century Roman Empire, men were allowed sexual freedom outside of marriage, while women were expected to be sexually chaste and modest. However, recognizing that both men and women are one in Christ (Gal. 3:28), Paul rejected this double standard and demanded the same obligations of husbands and wives in their marital sex. "Let the husband render to his wife the affection due her, and likewise also the wife to her husband" (1 Cor. 7:3).

If we look more closely at verse 4, which calls for husbands and wives to have authority over each other's bodies, we find a key principle of marital sex. When a wife does not have authority over her own body, but her husband does, it means that she is to give him complete control over her body. In other words, she should give herself to him when he wants her and treat him in a way that satisfies him in the bedroom. In the same way, a husband should not have authority over his own body, but should surrender it to his wife. That is, he is to be willing to give his own body to her when she wants it and to treat her in a way that satisfies her in the bedroom. In short, a couple should have marital sex that

---

★

67) 김세윤, 『하나님이 만드신 여성』 (서울: 두란노, 2004), 48.

satisfies each other. By satisfying each other sexually, they're actually satisfying their own desires. Of course, it would be great if they were both satisfied at the same time, but even if that's not the case, they should be able to take pleasure in seeing their spouse satisfied.

This is the way God the Trinity looks toward one another. God the Father delights in exalting God the Son. Likewise, the Son delights in giving Himself for the glory of the Father. God the Holy Spirit also delights to bear witness to the work of the Son and to glorify the Father. From eternity, the Father, the Son, and the Holy Spirit have completely loved, delighted in, and been completely satisfied with one another.

The love of the Triune God for one another overflowed to the point that man and woman were created in the image of God. The most obvious point where man and woman love and long for each other is in their sexual desire. Therefore, this sexual desire is to be used as a means of "worship" that reflects the image of God. Just as the Triune God satisfies one another with pure love, so too should a husband and a wife seek to satisfy each other's bodies and hearts by being sensitive to each other in pure love. We must believe that "sexual union, when done properly and in a mutually satisfying way, is a way for God to demonstrate great spiritual truths."[68] This beautiful marital sex should not be perceived as impure because it has been tainted by a distorted sexual culture.

Conversely, we should not be drawn into a fallen culture that portrays sex outside of marriage is portrayed as beautiful and romantic. We must never forget that our sexual desires and even our sexual lives are always related to God, who is at the apex of our covenant relationship.

A Couple Bearing the Image of God

Man was created in the image of God, male and female.[69] This means that to fully bear the image of God, neither man nor woman can be alone. In particular, through marriage, a man and a woman become one flesh, and together they bear the image of God. The most basic meaning of the image of God is that both men and women are to be God's vicarious rulers.[70] Therefore, it has to do with working together of the couple as one flesh to fulfill God's mission for the kingdom of God. First, let's look at the creation account in Genesis 1.

★

68) 휘트 부부, 『즐거움을 위한 성』 권영석 외 옮김 (서울: 한국기독학생회출판부, 2000), 21.

69) Of course, some people are born intersex, meaning that they are not clearly biologically male or female, which should be viewed as a rare biological variation (or defect) that occurred after Adam's sin.

70) 김세윤, 『하나님이 만드신 여성』 14-15.

26 Then God said, "Let Us make man in Our image, according to Our likeness; let them have dominion over the fish of the sea, over the birds of the air, and over the cattle, over all the earth and over every creeping thing that creeps on the earth." 27 So God created man in His *own* image; in the image of God He created him; male and female He created them. (Gen. 1:26-27)

Verses 26 and 27 emphasize that God created man in His image, but there's something a little unusual. In verse 26, God says "Let Us make man in Our image, according to Our likeness."[71] In other words, the one and only God is referring to Himself as "Our" in the plural. There are many interpretations of this, but the most common is that it reflects the *Threeness* of God.[72] However, verse 27 says, "God created man in His *own* image; in the image of God He created him." That is, God is now referring to Himself in the singular, "His." This can be seen as emphasizing the *Oneness* of God. In the span of just one verse, God alternates between plural and singular references to Himself. The existence of God the Trinity is revealed in verses 26-27.

In this image of God the Trinity, God created man as male and female and joined them together as a couple. A married couple,

★

71) Note that in Hebrew usage, the words *image* and *likeness* are used interchangeably. 한정건, 『성경주석 창세기』 (서울: 고신총회출판국, 2016), 56.

72) For a more detailed discussion, see 송병현, 『엑스포지멘터리 창세기』 87-88.

then, is a communal being that bears the image of God the Trinity. Just as the Trinity (Father, Son, and Holy Spirit) cannot exist without one of the Three Persons, neither can a married couple fully bear the image of God without their spouse. From the moment of marriage, a husband and wife become a "community of beings" who together reveal the image of God the Trinity. Just as God has both *Threeness* and *Oneness*, so a husband and wife exist as separate persons and yet form one flesh. Just as the Triune God refers to Himself as "Our" (plural) and "His" (singular), or "One," so the married couple refers to themselves as "our" and "one flesh." Love is the driving force that makes this state possible. Therefore, a married couple should strive to bear the image of God by loving each other. If there is a serious crisis between a couple and they despise each other, they are guilty of destroying the image of God.

And when we say that man is created in the image of God, we also mean that the attributes of God the Trinity include both masculinity and femininity. The term *femininity* of God may be misunderstood, but I'm going to use it according to the usage of one theologian.[73] God the Father and Jesus the Son are revealed as "male" in the Bible. This does not mean that we should equate Him with biological man. The infinite being of God cannot be

★
73) 송민원, "하나님의 여성성을 나타내는 "라함(םחٓ)"에 대한 묵상", Institute for Biblical Preaching, 2021년 8월 25일, https://ibp.or.kr/wordspostachio/?bmode=view&idx=7632817.

contained in a human male trapped in finitude. Interestingly, God the Holy Spirit is referred to by the feminine Hebrew noun *ruach* (רוח) in the Old Testament and the neuter Greek noun *pneuma* (πνεῦμα) in the New Testament. Of course, this is not biological sex, but gender as a grammatical element.

In any case, the variety of genders that refer to God's Persons shows that masculinity is not the only attribute of God. (Note that grammatical gender does not necessarily correspond to biological sex, but it is related to biological characteristics.) We also see glimpses of God's femininity in the way He embraces and loves His children without limits, holding them in His arms to the end.[74]

So we can think of the masculinity and femininity of a couple as collectively reflecting the image of God. In this context, neither husband nor wife has the upper hand in bearing the image of God. They stand in the full image of God when they are complementary to each other and bound together by the bonds of love. How do you perceive your spouse? Do you see him/her as a loving partner in bearing the image of God together?

Furthermore, when we say that a married couple bears the image of God, we mean that they bear the image of Christ in their marriage because Christ is the image of God (2 Cor. 4:4; Col. 1:15; Heb. 1:3). The image of Christ should be reflected in the marriage as a couple realizes how much Christ loves God and how much He loves His body, the Church. Therefore, how well a husband and wife bear the image of God depends on how much they love God and how much they love the church community. While a married couple is a community of beings who bear the image of God, we must not forget that the substance of that image is Christ, the Head of the church. In other words, a married couple does not bear the image of God themselves, but they bear the image of God through Christ, their eternal Bridegroom.

Christ is also the one through whom "the image of the invisible God" (Col. 1:15) has been made visible to our eyes. Likewise, a married couple with Christ as their Bridegroom shows the image of the invisible God to their neighbors through Christ. According to Ephesians 5:31-32, the image of Christ and the church should be revealed through the married couple, so when we say that a couple bears the image of God, we mean that they show what Christ and the church look like through their marriage. That is, the invisible image of God is made visible through the Christian couple, which is the mystical union of Christ and the church!

A Mutually Submissive Couple

There is a consideration to be made when reflecting the image of Christ and the church in marriage. While it is true that the relationship between a husband and wife reflects Christ and the church, the two do not always correspond in every way. We shouldn't approach it as a husband demanding unconditional submission from his wife because the husband corresponds to Christ and the wife corresponds to the church, and the church must submit to her head, Christ. Why is this? Because he is not Christ and she is not the church. While the Bible calls for a Christ-like role for husbands, we must also consider that husbands are imperfect sinners. In Ephesians 5, we find a passage about wives and husbands.

> 22 Wives, submit to your own husbands, as to the Lord. 23 For the husband is head of the wife, as also Christ is head of the church; and He is the Savior of the body. 24 Therefore, just as the church is subject to Christ, so *let* the wives *be* to their own husbands in everything. (Eph. 5:22-24)

Coincidentally, it begins with an exhortation that husbands will love. Wives are to submit to their husbands as they submit to the Lord, Paul explains, because the husband is the head of the wife, just as Christ is the head of the church. Therefore, he says, wives should submit to their own husbands in everything, just as the church submits to Christ.

At this point, Paul's exhortation might make today's wives feel uncomfortable. Husbands, on the other hand, may be more likely to cheer. However, we need to interpret and apply the Bible text correctly. First of all, this text is connected to the previous context. Paul is now exhorting the Ephesian church members on various aspects of what the church, the body of Christ, should be like. (Ephesians is the quintessential book on ecclesiology.) In Chapter 5, he exhorts them to be imitators of God and to walk in love, just as Christ loved you (vv. 1-2). He exhorts them to walk as children of light by fleeing from all iniquity (vv. 3-14), and to be filled with the Holy Spirit in wisdom and discernment, praising the Lord and giving thanks to God the Father (vv. 15-20). Then he adds, "Submit to one another out of reverence for Christ" (v. 21, NIV). In this context, the passage on wives and husbands follows.

Since wives and husbands are also members of the Ephesian church, we should assume that the previous exhortation still applies to them, and that the new exhortation (v. 22) is addressed to them. In particular, what does Paul say in the immediately preceding verse? "Submit to one another out of reverence for Christ" (v. 21, NIV). That is why Paul says, "Wives, submit to your own husbands, as to the Lord," assuming that they submit to one another out of reverence for Christ.

In particular, Paul addresses the wives first, perhaps because he wants the Ephesian church's submission to Christ to be more clearly demonstrated by their submission to their husbands. Rather than requiring wives to submit to their husbands, it may be a greater expectation of wives in Christ.

For married couples who submit to one another out of reverence for Christ, Paul specifically exhorts wives to submit to their husbands as to the Lord. What does "as to the Lord" mean here? Primarily, it means to submit absolutely to the Lord, not to their husbands. The word "as" means that the two are similar but not identical, meaning that a wife's submission to the Lord and her submission to her husband are similar but not identical.[75] That is why a wife must first submit absolutely to the Lord.

At this point, wives are responsible for discerning their husbands' spiritual state. What should she do if her husband is not submitting to the Lord and is engaged in the sins of the world? Should she submit to him unconditionally, as she submits to the Lord, or should she submit to him wisely, as it says, "Submit to one another out of reverence for Christ," helping him to submit to Him out of reverence for Christ? The counsel to "submit to your own husbands, as to the Lord" presupposes that they also submit to the Lord. Therefore, if a husband does not revere Christ and submit to the Lord, the wife's first priority should be to lead him to revere and submit to Christ, whom she does revere. Otherwise,

★

75) John Piper, *This Momentary Marriage*, 68.

if she submits unconditionally to her husband, she is guilty of idolatry, serving him more than Christ.

However, if wives whose husbands revere Christ do not submit, they should take Paul's counsel as the Word of God, "for the husband is head of the wife, as also Christ is head of the church." (I call this the *covenantal headship* of the husband.) Because Christ's headship expresses care and responsibility, not oppression and domination,[76] the husband's headship means that he cares for his wife and is responsible for her. Wives who do not submit to their husbands, even though they are Christ-fearing husbands who care for and are responsible for their wives, are in fact not submitting to their husbands, but to Christ.

Now Paul gives an exhortation that wives will cheer. "Husbands, love your wives, just as Christ also loved the church and gave Himself for her" (Eph. 5:25). Every Christian knows how much Christ loves the church. He loved it enough to sacrifice everything for it, even His life on the cross. Even now, Christ's love for the church continues through the Holy Spirit. It is an eternal love that never changes. His love for the church is a perfect love that never diminishes.

This is the kind of love that husbands are encouraged to show toward their wives. As we've discussed in detail before, men

★

76) 길성남, 『에베소서 어떻게 읽을 것인가』 (서울: 한국성서유니온, 2005), 424.

have a habit of reverting to their old ways after a while, when the love hormones stop being secreted. They find it hard to love their wives as passionately as they once did. The exhortation that God gives through Paul is a great remedy to this condition of husbands. Imitating Christ, the perfect model for husbands, he exhorts them to love their wives unconditionally, even to the point of giving their all. The excuse, "I can't love my wife that way until she does something to deserve it," doesn't work. Why is this? Because the church doesn't deserve the love of Christ until she does something to deserve it. The church will always fall short of what He sees, but He will still love her, sanctify her, and finally present her to Himself in glory (5:26-27).

Husbands, do you not want to imitate the eternal Bridegroom, who presents His bride, the Church, in this way? If a husband sustains such love for his wife, there is no reason for her not to submit. If a husband shows such pure love to his wife and she does not submit to him, then she is certainly in a stubborn state, neither revering Christ nor submitting to Him. In this case, as in the counsel to wives above, husbands should first seek to induce their wives to revere and submit to Christ.

In summary, the relationship between husband and wife is one of mutual submission. As the couple submits to Christ together out of reverence for Him, the wife is to submit to her husband as to the Lord, and the husband is to love his wife with all his heart as Christ loves the church. This is what it means to show your neighbor what Christ and the church are like in marriage. Isn't this what you want your marriage to be like?

✏️ Starting Point for Your Child's Education

In November 2020, an 8-episode Korean drama called "산후조리원" (*Postnatal Care Center*) aired on the tvN channel.[77] There's an interesting line in the drama where two characters are interviewing to hire a legendary babysitter. Ha Sun Park, who plays the role of Eun Jung Jo, says in a plaintive tone:

> You know the story: Two daughters, gold medal. One son and one daughter, silver. Two sons, no medal. And three sons, "neck medal." If you feel sorry for me and come to my house, I will treat you more like a mother than my real mother.[78]

It's a funny and sad story, but it shows how hard childcare can be. Just like Eun Jung Jo in the movie, my wife and I are a "neck

★

77) Actors Ji Won Eom, Ha Sun Park, Hye Jin Jang, and others. tvN, 「산후조리원」, 2020.11.02. ~ 2020.11.24., https://tvn.cjenm.com/ko/birthcare.

78) tvN drama, 「산후조리원」 episode 6, November 17, 2020, https://youtu.be/3PxbKS6ksQQ?si= TgrKGQxwyKaZ7UIc. I translated the Korean dialogue into English.

medal" couple with three sons. (In Korea, there's a humorous expression called "neck medal," which is a pun. It literally means a medal around the neck, but it's also a wordplay referring to the idea of hanging oneself. It means that raising three sons is so challenging.) We are often told that our sons are well-behaved compared to other families, but it's a lot of work for us (especially my wife). When my three sons were deeply involved in Taekwondo, they used to perform bizarre magic tricks at home, such as opening and closing the refrigerator door with their feet. Now that they're older, they're much more subdued than they used to be.

Christ and the church should be reflected in the way couples love each other, but this can be difficult when children are involved. After some time of marriage, the love hormones are exhausted and it is not easy for couples to love each other. But when a child is born, the love of the couple is lost and they have to fight a war over childcare. Instead of submitting to each other out of reverence for Christ, the husband struggles in his own way, and the wife struggles in hers, wondering how they can endure the anguish of childcare and parenting.

Neither did I. As I mentioned at the beginning of this book, my wife and I had serious childcare issues. To be more precise, my wife was struggling with solo childcare and I was struggling with my own distorted sense of mission and immersion in ministry. My absence from childcare and parenting, which should be a joint endeavor between husband and wife, caused the conflict to continue for some time. Under these circumstances, it is almost wishful thinking to expect a beautiful picture of wives submitting to their husbands and husbands loving their wives in submission to one another out of reverence for Christ.

Nevertheless, we must remember His Word that He wants the aspect of Christ and the church to be witnessed by the way a couple loves and is happy with each other. This is the starting point for childcare and parenting, because the first people to witness this aspect of a couple are the children born to them. It can be easy to keep God's love and happiness between just the two of you. But for that love and happiness to have greater meaning, it must be shared with the children entrusted to them.

It's similar to how the children of God are happy to share in the overflowing love of God the Trinity. Jesus wants us to enjoy the same love with which God loved Him (John 15:9; 17:26). The Holy Spirit also wants us to have the same joy that He has for us in our tribulations (1 Thess. 1:6). So when a couple who bear the image of the God the Trinity raises children, they are demonstrating to their children the love and joy of God that they experience.

You might ask, "How can you even think about that when the reality of raising children is so difficult?" But it is for this very reason that couples need to be more filled with God's love. When couples struggle with parenting, it's often not so much the parenting, but the way they treat each other. The younger the child, the more important the mother is in raising the child, and the husband's attitude toward his wife and the way he speaks to her has a great impact on the relationship. Only when he is filled with God's love can he rightly love his wife, who is exhausted and sensitive from childcare, and participate in childcare together. This is actually a self-reflective confession. In the past, when my wife was struggling with childcare, instead of being filled with God's love, I was overwhelmed with my ministry and became even more exhausted and sensitive to her than she was. Although childcare and parenting is hard work, it can be hard but rewarding if the couple communicates well and is filled with God's love. For specifics on biblical childcare and parenting, see the writings of other experts.

Anyway, the point of this article is that the starting point for educating children (childcare and parenting) is to see Christ and the church reflected in the way a couple loves each other. In other words, when children see their father truly love their mother, they learn in a practical way how Jesus loves the church. And when children see their mother submit to their father out of reverence for Christ, they are actually learning how we, as the church, are to obey God. We may think they are not watching, but they are watching how their parents treat each other. They see how much their parents love God and are close to the Bible.

I am no exception in that regard. I often try to show my children that I love God and love His Word. I often tell them how happy I am to read and memorize the Bible. And unlike before, I often show my wife how much I love her in front of them. I try to let my three boys know how rewarding and happy their dad's ministry for the Lord is. One day, my oldest son, who is in junior high school, came home from the church retreat and told me about his dream.

Dad, I want to be a pastor like you.

At that moment, my wife and I were so happy and blessed his decision. I want to believe that the Lord has called him to be a pastor because he hasn't changed his mind about it since then. In his eyes, he is happy to see his dad loving God and doing missionary work with his mom. I will pray and watch to see how God will lead him in the future. In any case, I hope that seeing their mom and dad living happily and loving each other will help my three sons realize more about who Jesus is and what His beloved church is like.

1. Restate what it means to say that the marital sex renews the marriage covenant.

2. Do you want your needs to be satisfied first in the bedroom? Or do you make a conscious effort to satisfy your spouse first? Have an honest conversation about what you and your spouse each want and what you want to hear in response.

3. What efforts should couples make to bear the image of God? (You may base your answer on the material in this chapter.)

4. Do you think your children can learn about who Jesus is and what His beloved church looks like through your marriage? Talk about what you and your spouse want to do to show them that.

NaNCHAPTER 7

Real-Life Situations
with Bickering

Fervent in Faith but Often Fight

Failure Even When Faith Is Fervent

A Very Wise Husband

Man Cave Time

A Couple Navigating Menopause Wisely

Men's Language vs. Women's language

Need for Recognition, a Sense of Empathy

Ability to Fight and Reconcile Wisely

Tears Shed while Looking into the Face

A Wife Putting No Hope in Her Husband

God Alone Is Not Enough

♡ Fervent in Faith but Often Fight

There is a couple in their 40s who are fervent in their faith. The wife is especially passionate about prayer, seeking the guidance of the Holy Spirit in everything she does. Her husband is also passionate about his faith. The problem is that they often fight. The husband criticizes his wife's faith and speaks too harshly to her. For example, he says things like, "I love that you pray so hard, but you need to prove it with your life." She fights back and says, "You're reacting to me that way because your faith is still young." This is what her children often say:

Why are Mom and Dad always fighting about your faith in Jesus?

It's an unusual case of a couple having a lot of fights even though they are fervent in their faith. However, the problem is not their faith, but the way they treat each other. The wife prayed harder and asked for grace to become more indifferent to her husband's cruel words. One day she began to have compassion and not react to his attitude. But that's what worried me. Of course, it would be best if the husband immediately corrected his attitude and tone of voice and became more like his wife, but the atmosphere during the counseling session was that his attitude had not yet changed much. Moreover, the wife's attitude seemed to be that she just ignored him. In my eyes, it reads as the leeway of one who has received greater grace from God. If this continues, this couple will become even more disconnected. The wife may be hardened to her husband's cruel words because she feels she has received grace, but this very hardening may reinforce his words.

Isn't it ironic? She certainly prays and responds with grace, but her husband is more sensitive to her lack of listening to him. A person of good faith should always be aware of such things, especially in a marriage. In the case of someone who is being unreasonably hard on you, you may be able to keep your distance, but your marriage will not be restored if either of you is restored. Of course, it would be nice if a special grace came and dramatically restored the other one, but in general, the couple should talk to each other and work together to restore their relationship.

Otherwise, you may cut off communication with your spouse and become even more obsessed with your own prayer practice. While it's good to pour out your heart to God, if you use prayer or worship as a way to escape from your spouse, you could end up with a religious addiction. God is not pleased with prayer and worship when it's done without a restored relationship with your spouse. I know this was true for me 12 years ago. Meditate seriously on God's desire to see Christ and the church reflected in the way a husband and wife love each other.

⬭ Failure Even When Faith Is Fervent

There are times when a fervent faith can lead to a marriage in crisis. I once counseled a woman in her mid-40s named Elizabeth. She was an acquaintance of mine and a woman of great faith. As a pastor's daughter, she prayed every day and sincerely sought God's guidance. When she prayed for a spouse, she received God's answer and began a relationship that eventually developed into a serious relationship and marriage after she received a clear "sign" from God.

But during the marriage, problems began to arise. Whenever her husband received a salary, he would send it to his parents without discussing it with her. At first, she thought that her in-laws had something they couldn't tell her. But they took her son's filial piety for granted and treated her daughter-in-law roughly. Her husband's terrible behavior continued after that, so one day she asked me for counseling.

> Pastor, I think I had no understanding of men. I really got my prayers answered, we started dating and got married with a clear sign from God, but I really didn't know my husband was like this. My mom told me that if I just have faith and hold on, he will change, but how long should I hold on? It's been seven years now.

I used to know her as an elegant and proud woman, but due to the stress of her marriage, she had become a completely different person. She blamed herself for this because she hadn't been praying hard enough and lacked faith for the past seven years. She despaired that she was not fully submitting to her husband as the Bible says she should. She was especially troubled by the fact that both of her parents were pastor couples.

As I listened to her marriage story, I felt really hard. I couldn't help but think about how she had to manage the household without her husband's support. First of all, I could see that having a fervent faith does not necessarily correlate with a happy marriage. I realized that even if a woman has a fervent faith, she may have no understanding of men and her marriage may fail. There are more people like that than you think. So what do you think they need?

First, even if they love God with a burning faith, they still need to be disciplined in how they learn about and love the opposite sex. It may seem that realizing the gospel and loving God passionately will enable you to know and love the opposite sex well, but this is often not the case. It is easy to assume that he/she loves God on the same level that you love God. Furthermore, men tend to hide their true selves during a relationship and try to fit in with the woman as much as possible, which makes it difficult for women to get to know them until marriage.

That's why women like Elizabeth need to listen and learn about what men are like from different people and situations. Don't rely too much on your own spiritual sense. People who pray a lot and claim to have a strong faith are less likely to listen to the advice of those around them. The idea is that when you pray, God will guide you and show you signs. Sometimes this is true, but there are many times when it is not, especially when it comes to marriage.

Second, there is a balance to be struck when practicing the command to submit to your husbands (Eph. 5:22). I have previously provided a detailed exegesis of this verse. The guiding principle in applying this verse in marriage is: "Are you submitting to each other out of reverence for Christ together?" The first thing to do is to examine whether either the husband or the wife is in full submission to Christ. Reverence for Christ means strict obedience to His Word. In this state, by submitting to one another, especially wives, should submit to their husbands as to the Lord.

In the case of Elizabeth, her husband was not in such a state. A Christ-fearing husband is supposed to love his wife as his own body, but her husband was only showing filial piety to his parents, without any consideration for his wife's situation and emotional state. This is especially true when a man has not left his parents, as emphasized earlier. According to Genesis 2:24, a man is supposed to leave his parents when he marries and become emotionally and relationally independent so that he can fully unite with his wife, and Elizabeth's husband completely failed in this regard.

Anyway, I counseled her appropriately with what I have said in this article and prayed for her. At that time, she even thought of getting a divorce, but fortunately, years later, her relationship with her husband has been restored, and her in-laws no longer treat her daughter-in-law as badly as they used to. This is thanks to the Lord's love and grace for her.

A Very Wise Husband

I once had a conversation with a couple in their 60s about their marriage. They seemed to be doing really well and were very happy compared to other couples their age. Not because of their faith, but because of their marriage in general, and the husband in particular was a model husband, which is hard to find in the 60s. I began to wonder about his relationship with his parents and how he grew up. Naturally, I assumed that his family was functional, but it was not at all what I expected. He grew up with strict parents, especially his mother. Older Korean mothers are usually very attached to their sons, and she was one of them. Even when he got married, he would visit his mother every week and stay overnight, but he would put his wife in another room and he would have to sleep with her mother. Since his father was dead, he was his mother's "psychological spouse."[79]

At that moment, I started to get a little chill. It's a rare situation for young couples these days. It must have been very difficult for the son to have such a mother, but also for the daughter-in-law to have to live with such a son. Moreover, his mother always treated her badly. When the son lost weight, she blamed her for starving him (which wasn't true), and when he got sick, she kept nagging her, saying that it was because she was causing him a lot of trouble. One day, the son mustered up the courage to say in a polite tone something to his mother in front of her daughter-in-law.

Mother, from now on, you will see what a good person your daughter-in-law is.

His answer sounded very wise. At that moment I remembered my late father. My father was in the same situation, but he was a man with a bad temper and often fought with my grandmother. Maybe it was because he had no faith. My grandmother's excessive attachment to my father eventually caused my mother to run away from home. They are both dead now, but thanks to them, I was able to experience a dysfunctional family firsthand.

★

79) 황지영, 『사이좋은 부모생활』 (서울: 아르카, 2022), 109.

In such a situation, many counselors would advise their clients to say firmly, "Don't mess with my woman!" This may be the most effective way to deal with the situation, but it will inevitably hurt the mother. Such shock therapy is sometimes necessary to correct the distorted love for her son.

However, the man's answer above presented a great challenge to both his mother and his wife without hurting either of them. First, he didn't blatantly take his wife's side in front of his mother, and he didn't shield his mother from his wife. He said that her mother kept thinking of her daughter-in-law as a bad person, but she would realize that this was not the case when she saw her daughter-in-law's behavior.

Indeed, a remarkable change took place after that. The daughter-in-law became much nicer to her mother-in-law than she had been before, and she did everything in her power to show her how well she served and cared for her husband. The mother-in-law's heart was opened and she began to see her daughter-in-law differently, and now, more than 20 years later, the relationship is well restored in the gospel. For a man in his 60s who grew up in a dysfunctional family, he is very wise and has a successful marriage. As he confessed, the restoration was possible because he properly experienced God's love through the Holy Spirit.

♡ Man Cave Time

A newlywed couple I've officiated at before came to me short-ly after their wedding. I noticed that the atmosphere was differ-ent than before the wedding. During a meal, the bride spoke in a slightly upset voice.

> Pastor, I think my husband has changed since we got married. When he comes home from work, he doesn't want to talk to me, he just stares at his cell phone for a while and zones out.

At that moment, I remembered my old self: I would come home from the ministry, relaxed, dazed, and unable to do anything but be alone. I was often scolded and misunderstood by my wife. It took us a long time to understand each other.

We need to know some of the differences in temperament be-tween men and women. In general, men like to have what's called "cave time" when they come home from a long day at work. What this means is that their minds and bodies are tense and rigid from their workday, and when they get home, they're in their most re-laxed state, where their whole body relaxes and they want to be still for a while. Women, on the other hand, usually come home after being out and about, and try to relieve the stress and tension of the day by talking to their families. (Of course, there are men and women with opposite temperaments.) This difference in temperament is why couples often misunderstand each other in the early stages of marriage.

Wives are happy to see their husbands come home and want to spend time catching up on the day's events. However, when husbands come home, they tend to drop everything and just hang out for a while. These days, it's more often than not, they're looking at their phones. This is where couples start to misunderstand each other. The wife is happy to see her husband and wants to talk to him, but he keeps trying to keep to himself, so she feels rejected, and she thinks he's changed since they got married.

The husband never wants to be alone because he doesn't like his wife, so he feels a little bit guilty about it. If she leaves him alone when he gets home, he'll wake up later and approach her, but she can't wait for that time and starts bothering him about why he keeps trying to be alone. The husband gets frustrated again and starts yelling at her, asking why she can't just leave him alone. She gets angry again, saying that she really doesn't understand, and closes the door and goes inside. At this moment, the husband finds it hard to understand her behavior, and at the same time, he begins to blame himself for wanting to be alone.

This was the case for me and my wife. Many couples experience this vicious cycle of conflict early in their marriage. Wives need to allow their husbands some cave time (30 to 60 minutes).

It's actually wise to let him go into his cave when he comes home and stay there for a while, and then he'll crawl out on his own. He's completely over it now, as if nothing ever happened. If you start nagging your husband to stop him from going into the cave, the stress of your nagging will only prolong his cave time. If wives want to nag their husbands about why men are so selfish, they should be patient and understand that it's just the way they are.

The same goes for raising children. Boys usually come home from school and want to lie around doing nothing, but it's good for mom's mental health to leave them alone for a while. If you start nagging them to get cleaned up, they will get annoyed with you. Of course, if they're too engrossed in their phones or smart devices to do anything else, they're already past cave time and want to keep indulging, so you have to be firm and cut them off. Dads, being men, know why their sons are like that, so they just watch with bated breath. Men are so simple, after all. Even in the field of psychology, there is female psychology and child psychology, but there is no male psychology. Why is this? Because it's the same as child psychology.

♡A Couple Navigating Menopause Wisely

I know another couple in their 60s. Sometimes I ask them for advice. The husband is very active and outgoing. He has the gift of easily talking to strangers and, after a while, turning them into friends. The wife, on the other hand, is relatively calm and obedient to her husband, and her emotions don't usually change much. Although she often feels overwhelmed by his sudden actions and words, she has been living with them. She always thinks and acts in line with her husband's ideas and positions, especially considering his social position. As a result, suppressing her feelings has become a habit, and she has come to recognize it as her true state.

But the problem started when she got older. The symptoms of menopause hit hard. All the emotions she had tolerated exploded at once. (Husbands should be warned that this can happen even to Christians!) She began to make it her life's goal to make her husband suffer, and if he offended her in the slightest way, she would lash out at him without explanation, leaving him bewildered and unfamiliar with a wife who had never been the same. As with all couples, husbands are stronger when they are younger, but as they age, hormonal reversals occur, and men become more feminized and women more masculine. In any case, the husband was very troubled by his wife's ongoing menopausal symptoms, but he began to cope with them with his characteristic wit. One day, when his wife had another outburst and started attacking him, he said:

Honey, this is so exciting! Do it one more time!

At that moment, the wife was so taken aback that she was at a loss for words: when she exploded and attacked her husband, she wanted him to suffer, but now that he suddenly said he liked it, she didn't want to do it anymore. Why is that? Because if he liked it, then she would lose her goal in life, which was to make him suffer. She thought that would make her feel worse.

I laughed out loud at her menopause story, but I thought it was really wise. I think I'll try it on my wife when I'm in that situation sooner or later. Of course, there's no guarantee that she'll react the same way, but I'm willing to take a chance and give it a try. I can't help but wonder, what if an even stronger backlash arises as a result?

Men's Language vs. Women's language

Men and women use different languages. Men are primarily focused on conveying information, whereas women put deeper meanings and intentions into their words. In other words, men are more factual, while women are more emotional. This also means that each remembers differently through language. Communication and memory can never be separated. Men tend to remember what they communicate in the form of information, while women tend to remember it in the form of emotions.

These differences cause both big and small problems between couples. When a husband has a conflict, he tends to think that once the facts of the situation are explained, that's all there is to it, and he doesn't want to worry too much about the emotional issues. Wives, on the other hand, want the facts to be clear and hope that any lasting emotional issues will be resolved. Otherwise, she'll keep bringing up things that happened a long time ago in every argument, and she wants to keep pushing him. The husband has long since moved on and doesn't even remember what happened, but the wife's feelings are still hurt because it is imprinted on her heart.

If the situation becomes more serious and persistent, it can quickly lead to a divorce. This is a real-life story of a couple whose children were all married and living on their own, and one day the wife asked her husband for a divorce. The husband couldn't understand why she wanted a divorce because they had had some conflicts in the past, but they hadn't lasted long and he didn't think they were serious. But as it turned out, she'd been putting up with it all along. She'd been trying to talk to him, but he wouldn't listen to her, so she'd been pushing her feelings aside for the sake of the children and waiting for an opportunity to get a divorce. Husbands who can't read their wives' hearts should beware.

For a while, I struggled with not understanding women's language. Nowadays, I'm almost like a new man, but in the past, my inability to understand my wife's words often led to conflicts. The conversation would go something like this:

"What a selfish husband you are!"

"What? Why am I being selfish?"

"You don't know that?"

"Of course I don't know, you have to tell me."

For a while, I got really angry whenever my wife called me selfish, because everyone I meet tells me that I'm selfless and don't seem to care much about myself. The husbands, who still don't understand what's wrong now, are someone who doesn't understand women's language like I used to. I got caught up in my wife's word "selfish" and spent a lot of time defending myself, saying that I'm definitely not that kind of person. But when she said that, she was asking me to spend some time with her and not just spend time with myself, so she was using the word "selfish" to express her intention and hidden meaning.

At first, I didn't understand why she was expressing herself that way. I wondered why she would use such euphemisms when it would be clearer to just say what she really wanted. But it turns out it's because men's language is different from women's. Or, to put it another way, women need to understand men's language. Women often complain that men are frustrating, and that's because of this difference. So if wives want to get their husbands, and especially their sons, to move, they need to make eye contact and speak clearly. Otherwise, they'll have a hard time understanding what you're saying. Of course, husbands who understand women's language do a great job.

The difference in language between men and women is also evident when it comes to work. Men are more likely to be able to put aside their feelings about someone who offends them and just do their job. This is because men tend to communicate with facts rather than emotions. Of course, when they finish their work, they may take out their feelings by cursing the person out of sight. Women, on the other hand, find it very difficult to work with someone who makes them feel bad. Once their feelings are hurt, they have a hard time communicating with the person, not only in the workplace but also with the person themselves. This is because women are emotionally driven.

In any case, even Christian couples need to understand the language differences between men and women in order to have a smooth marriage. No matter how much a couple dreams of the kingdom of God together and tries to live out their holy mission, it is very difficult if they continue to have conflicts in such daily matters. This is actually a story of my own failure in the past. God wants us to understand, care for, and be happy with each other in our daily lives before we think about big discourses and do big things. But how well do husbands understand their wives' language, and how often do wives express themselves in a way that their husbands understand?

♡ Need for Recognition, a Sense of Empathy

Chang Ok Kim, a famous Korean communication lecturer, said that husbands don't want love, but recognition and praise.[80] He said that wives can tell when they say to their husbands, "Honey, I love you!" When husbands hear the words "I love you," they become anxious and wonder if they've done something wrong. That's a pretty valid analysis. Of course, this analysis probably applies mainly to couples who have been married for a long time. Newlyweds, still full of love hormones, routinely say "I love you!" to each other.

In general, men have a stronger need for recognition and women have a stronger sense of empathy. This is even more true for married couples. Husbands usually want to be recognized by their wives, even if they don't get it from other people. This is true in my own case. I have relatively high self-esteem, and I don't pay much attention to what other people say to me. Unless it's advice

★

80) 새롭게하소서CBS, "소통이 안 되면? 고통이 온다! 소통 전문가 김창옥 강사", 2021년 9월 8일, https://youtu.be/xGO2EdmVPic?si=L5M22pF3CkL78k5o.

that comes from someone who really cares about me, I let it go in one ear and out the other. But strangely enough, I'm very sensitive to what my wife says. I don't mind when someone else evaluates my lectures or sermons, but when my wife gives me a review, every single word is vividly connected to my self-esteem. If other people's recognition and praise is a 10 for me, my wife's recognition and praise is a 100+.

But why do men have such a strong need for recognition? There are many theories, but the best explanation is that God gave men this tendency. This need for recognition is especially evident in the bedroom, where masculinity and femininity are on full display. At the end of their relationship, a husband will often ask his wife, "How was your night?" because he wants to be recognized for his sexual attractiveness and ability. If she answers "Not so good," his self-esteem drops, and it's important for wives to answer wisely.

It also seems that God's giving men the responsibility of caring for the home is connected to men's need for recognition, because recognition and praise follow a job well done. Therefore, wives should often recognize and praise their husbands for their hard work for the family. Wives should stop thinking that they have to do something to be praised. Instead, please say, "My husband is the best!" even if it's not enough. Praise and recognition from a wife is the best kind of love for a husband who feels inadequate and hopeless. If you withhold praise because you're afraid it will make him arrogant, you shouldn't be. Most husbands don't become arrogant because of their wife's praise. In fact, wives of arrogant husbands don't usually praise their husbands because they are arrogant by nature. If you think your husband is not an arrogant person, please praise him without hesitation.

One of the best ways for wives to get their husbands moving is through recognition and praise. If you praise your husband for cleaning the house, he'll probably spend the rest of the day running back and forth with the vacuum cleaner. It's been said that "praise makes the whale dance," but I guess the whale is a male. It was said in jest, but the point is that praise has a positive response and effect. Wives may protest, "I'm raising a big boy," but the reality is that men become big boys when they get married. On the other hand, when a woman gets married, she seems to become a wife and a mother at the same time. Somehow I feel sorry for the wives because they seem to lose out.

Women have a strong sense of empathy, and this ability doesn't seem to change after marriage. This, too, can be understood in terms of God's design for women. God created woman to be a helper for Adam (Gen. 2:18), and empathy is essential for a wife to help her husband. She was to be a supportive and empathetic partner in Adam's mission.

In couples counseling, the husband is often the "perpetrator" and the wife the "victim," and yet wives often want to empathize and understand their husbands. I once counseled a newlywed couple. The husband grew up in a dysfunctional family and had severe emotional deficits, while the wife grew up in a relatively healthy environment. After a while, the husband's erratic behavior began to show up. He would verbally abuse her for not meeting his standards, and when he couldn't control his emotions, he would even resort to physical violence. His wife was so alarmed by his behavior that she even considered divorce and went to her parents' house to escape for a while. However, she was worried about him and tried to empathize with him, and fortunately, their relationship recovered well.

Women have a strong sense of empathy and crave to be empathized with. That's why husbands should often use empathic language with their wives. In the past, I wasn't very good at using empathy with my wife. Like most men, I focused on problem solving rather than empathy. When my wife told me that she was feeling sick, I was immature in how I talked to her:

"Honey, I don't think I'm feeling well."

"Let's see a doctor right away."

"I say I'm sick and you don't even ask if I'm okay?"

"Of course, that's why I said let's see a doctor first."

I have tried to overcome my immaturity in many ways. As a result of growing up in a dysfunctional family, my empathy and expressive skills were severely lacking. At the advice of a counselor, I wrote down empathetic words on paper and read them to my wife. The advice is that if you can't think of something empathetic to say on the spot, try that way. It felt really awkward and weird, but after a few tries, I was able to empathize with my wife's feelings with appropriate words depending on the situation.

In fact, a sense of empathy is essential for both husbands and wives. They just have different points of empathy. Husbands need to empathize with their wives' feelings and moods to feel more loved. Wives need to empathize with the work their husbands do, which is a form of recognition and praise for them. So, from the husband's point of view, empathy from his wife is another expression of recognition.

Ability to Fight and Reconcile Wisely

What does it mean to say that a couple has a good relationship? Does a couple has a good relationship if they never fight? Maybe, but I don't think it's a good idea to judge a couple by the number of fights they have. A couple that never fights is more likely to be in crisis, because one of them is often holding on for dear life. A sentence from the British playwright A. P. Herbert (1890-1971) gives us a profound insight. "The concept of two people living together for 25 years without a serious dispute suggests a lack of spirit only to be admired in sheep."[81]

So we should understand the term "a good relationship" to mean "the ability to fight and reconcile wisely." To use a specific term, a good relationship is characterized by high resilience. In Korea, the concept of resilience was first proposed by Professor Joo Hwan Kim of Yonsei University in 2011, and is defined as "the ability to use all kinds of adversities and difficulties that come your way as a springboard to leap forward."[82] It's a concept which is used in general studies, but I think we can benefit from reinterpreting it. As Christians, we have "spiritual resilience" basically. In other words, because we are in Christ, we have the power of the Holy Spirit to lift us up in the midst of adversity. But enjoying this is on another level.

Christians should be able to fight wisely in marital quarrels and be reconciled at the same time. The power of reconciliation through the cross is inherent in those who believe in the gospel. No matter how badly a husband and wife fight, there is nothing that cannot be reconciled in Christ. It is the love of the cross that enables us to love even our enemies, and spouses who are married in love can certainly be reconciled more easily than enemies. A cou-

★

81) BrainyQuote, "A. P. Herbert Quotes," accessed December 17, 2024, https://www.brainyquote.com/quotes/a_p_herbert_106679.
82) 김주환, 『회복탄력성』 (고양: 위즈덤하우스, 2011), 17.

ple once told me that they had gone beyond the level of forgiveness that was commanded in Matthew 18:22. No matter how much the wife hated her husband, she was to forgive him "seventy-seven times" (Matt. 18:22, ESV). She said that she believed in Jesus, but she could never forgive her husband. While I sympathize with her unspeakable pain, we can't apply Jesus' words in this way.

Christian couples have certain boundaries that they must honor even when they fight. Under no circumstances should you maliciously attack your spouse's faith or use physical or emotional violence against him/her. Attacking your spouse's faith is a demonstration of your own faith because, as you know, it is through marriage that Christ and the church are demonstrated, and by attacking your spouse's faith, you are confessing that you are demonstrating Christ and the church on that level. If you criticize your spouse's faith, you are simultaneously criticizing your own faith, which is one with his/her, and it is in this state that the aspect of Christ and the church is revealed. The faith of a married couple is meant to grow together, and it is impossible in principle for one to be superior to the other. They are no longer two, but one flesh.

Also, Christian couples should never use violence against each other! This includes emotional violence (or abuse) as well as physical violence. In fact, this is a basic ethic that applies to all people, not just Christians. Physical violence is a shameless act because it destroys the body of Christ with one's own hands.

There are a surprising number of abusive husbands, even among Christians. Even among pastoral couples. When the husband comes home from the ministry because of its stress, he may argue unnecessarily with his wife and become violent. In such cases, they should be temporarily isolated.

Even if it's not physical violence, emotional violence is never okay. In some ways, emotional violence (or abuse) can be more frightening than physical violence. It's often a husband who uses verbal abuse to create an atmosphere of fear in order to make his wife obey him, even gaslighting her into believing that she is the cause of the violence. This destroys the personality of the partner, who is already dominated by him and constantly justifies his behavior because she thinks she is the cause of everything that happens. If it gets to this point, a third party must step in and take action.

It's also important to make sure that you both understand that the purpose of fighting is to resolve the conflict and reconcile. If you're not a couple, in extreme cases you can fight like you'll never see each other again. But if you are a couple, you can't stay in conflict because you have to live together unless you get divorced. Therefore, it is in the best interest of both parties to resolve the conflict and reconcile as soon as possible, if you have to reconcile. In this case, Christian couples should trust the Holy Spirit to reconcile them. In the Holy Spirit, the husband and wife were already united as the body of Christ before they were married. Furthermore, from the moment they are married, they are members of the body of Christ in a way that distinguishes them from others. The relationship between husband and wife is even likened to the relationship between Christ and the church.

If so, then the fact that the couple remains in conflict without reconciliation means that Christ and the church are seen as being in constant discord. Christ and the church cannot be at odds under any circumstances because the church is the body of Christ. Therefore, even if a couple's pride is hurt, they should resolve the conflict and reconcile quickly for the sake of our Lord. In the past, my wife and I often said to each other after a fight:

Nevertheless, I love you because of God.

And then, strangely enough, we felt much better, and we suddenly felt a surge of remorse, and we realized that we should be nicer to each other from now on.

♡ Tears Shed while Looking into the Face

A couple in their 50s was facing divorce. Unlike when they were newlyweds, the husband liked to drink and his temper had become unruly, hitting and verbally abusing his wife. The wife, not to be outdone, resisted him, but at some point she just put up with it. Somehow, she managed to grit her teeth and put up with it until her children became adults. One day, she blatantly asked him for a divorce, and he couldn't take it anymore and filed for divorce.

The day has come for them to make a final statement to their lawyer. The lawyer asked the couple to go into separate rooms and reminisce about the past for 10 minutes. He told them to think of as many good and bad memories as they could of each other during their life together and then come back. The lawyer asked the couple what they thought about during the 10 minutes, and they said that they could only think of bad memories of each other. This time, he asked them to look each other in the face for three minutes and try to make eye contact. The husband and wife felt incredibly awkward, but they thought it would be the last time and looked into each other's eyes. After a little while, the wife suddenly burst into tears and started sobbing. The lawyer asked her why she suddenly started crying.

I don't know how long it's been since I've looked at my husband's face this closely. His face didn't look like this, and the wrinkles that have appeared remind me of all the hard work he has done to feed his family.

This time, the husband started crying as well. The lawyer asked him why.

My wife was crying, so I cried along with her.

That day, the couple stopped thinking about divorce and rebuilt their relationship. The tears they shed as they looked at each other's faces triggered the healing power. In this way, the tears have the power to heal inner wounds. Of course, God does the underlying healing of the heart. But tears serve as a channel for God's work. While non-Christians experience the relief of sobbing, we experience with it the comfort of heaven through our tears.

When was the last time you looked into your spouse's face and made eye contact with him/her? Do you feel uncomfortable making eye contact with your spouse and suffer from an unexplained emptiness? What if you made eye contact with him/her more often, remembering the good times you had together?

♡ A Wife Putting No Hope in Her Husband

At the beginning of this book, there is a foreword by my wife. In the last paragraph she says, "Let us no longer put our hope in our husbands, but only in the Lord." She doesn't just say it, she really thinks and says it. My wife is very dependent on her husband. I, on the other hand, am very independent. I've never felt lonely when I'm alone.

I didn't realize it when I was dating, but it became a problem in my marriage. My burning sense of mission led me to believe that if I immersed myself in my ministry, my wife would be able to independently raise and nurture the children. I've previously covered in detail how this can be a slippery slope to workaholism. In any case, while my wife struggled with my independent temperament, she gradually began to reach a remarkable state. It means that she no longer puts her hope in her husband.

You may think this is a bizarre statement, but to my surprise, my wife loves and respects her husband more than ever before. These are her words, not mine. She says that she no longer puts her hope in her husband, and strangely enough, he seems lovable now. Why is this? I think she responds because her heart is freed up by relying on the Lord and putting her hope in the Lord, not in her husband. She puts her hope in the Lord and prays hard for her husband. With her heart at ease, she rarely nags her husband. If her husband offends her, she "snitches" right to God and uses the power of prayer to make him repent.

I like this kind of wife and I love her. Her dependence on me is still strong, but she is not as dependent on me as she used to be. Because she is more dependent on God and treats me with a heart given by the Holy Spirit, she is not as discouraged as before when her expectations of me are not fulfilled. She knows that her true comfort and hope is in God, not in her husband.

Before getting married, she prayed to find a husband who loved God more than her. Then she met such a man and her heart was troubled for a while. Of course, this does not mean that I literally do not love my wife, but only God. I have discussed in detail how loving God and loving our spouse are inseparable. Nevertheless, until 12 years ago, I neglected to love my wife because of a distorted sense of mission. While there was a "positive" aspect to this, in that my wife put her hope in God rather than in her husband, looking back now, I regret that she must have suffered because of her husband who "loved" God more than her. In the future, I think I should try harder to make her put her hope in her husband as well.

God Alone Is Not Enough

We must love God more, but we cannot love God alone. What I mean is, it is impossible to reject all people and "only" love God. Even those who are filled with the Holy Spirit and love God will have a longing to be with their fellow workers and to see people. The apostle Paul, who loved God more than anyone else, longed to see Timothy (2 Tim. 1:4) and to be with his fellow workers.

There is a place in everyone's heart that only God can fill, but there is also a place that God fills through people. This place in the heart cannot be filled by God alone without going through people. Do you think that if you pray hard enough, all the places in your heart will be filled with God's love? Not at all. Of course we have to pray hard, but the comfort and love that God gives through people really works in our hearts. Humans are relational by nature. Just as God the Father, the Son, and the Holy Spirit exist in the *relationship* of the Trinity, we exist and interact with Christians united in Christ, and it is in this relationship that God's love fills our hearts.

Nowhere is this principle more evident than in the marriage relationship. A husband and a wife each have a place in their hearts that only God can fill, but at the same time, there is a place for God to fill the heart of the wife through the husband and for God to fill the heart of the husband through the wife. This is why a married couple should love each other. Each must be filled with God's love. In this state, when they love each other, the love of God that is poured into their hearts flows into each other. This is how God fills the heart of the wife through the husband and the heart of the husband through the wife.

I love God, but I can't love God alone without my wife, because my wife and I are one flesh. I am satisfied with God alone, but my satisfaction is much greater when I am loved by my wife. No matter how much I love God, there is a place in my heart that is not filled. Married couples know intuitively what this is. No matter how much you love God alone, if you are not loved by your spouse, there is a place in your heart that is not filled, because through the *relationship* of marriage, God's love should flow to each other, but it does not.

In any case, we must recognize that there is a place in our hearts that is not filled by God alone. A husband needs the love of his wife to fill the place in his heart. Likewise, a wife needs the love of her husband to fill the place in her heart. If you do not fill the place in your spouse's heart, it may be filled by the love of another. So if your spouse says, "I'm satisfied with God alone," you may need to look closely at what your spouse really means.

Questions for Sharing and Application

1. Share honestly what you usually argue about when you have a fight.

2. How do you react when your husband is in the cave time? Or how do you react when your wife tries to pull you out of the cave?

3. Have you ever felt frustrated in a conversation with your spouse? And if so, what was it that you didn't understand each other?

4. How do you usually reconcile when you have a fight? Or do you just try to avoid conflict whenever it arises? Share with each other how you can reconcile better.

CHAPTER 8

Divorce, Remarriage, and Reality

🎁 A Boy Growing Up in a Divorced Family

There was a couple who were fighting every day. The conflict between the mother-in-law and daughter-in-law caused a crisis in their relationship. Their child, who was born in the meantime, sensed that something was wrong in the house when he entered elementary school. He even witnessed his father beating his mother to a bloody pulp. The domestic violence and verbal abuse showed no signs of stopping. One day, his father collapsed from his heart disease, and his mother decided that she had her chance and ran away from home, abandoning her children and choking back tears.

He was originally an outgoing person, but due to a terrible home environment, he became increasingly anxious, obsessive, and closed off. He suffered from a fluency disorder (severe stuttering) that left him unable to communicate with people. The good news is that when her father collapsed and was sick in bed for 14 years, he attended church to help him cope with the adversity. His life could have been ruined by a dysfunctional family, but God took hold of him and molded him into the pastor who is writing this book.[83]

Originally, I wanted to avoid the grim subject of divorce in *A*

★

83) For more information, see 권율, 『전능자의 손길』 (서울: 세움북스, 2024).

Theology for Married Couples. But there are a surprising number of couples in the church who are contemplating or actually divorcing. So, as someone who grew up in a real divorced family, I want to address the issue of divorce in a simple way. I want to speak in experiential language about the terrible consequences of divorce for both parties and their children. I hope that couples who are contemplating divorce in their hearts will listen carefully.

Above all, divorce is a terrible offense because it breaks the marriage covenant that they made before God. I sometimes officiate at weddings. When a bride and groom make their marriage vows before a God-ordained officiant, they solemnly swear to honor that covenant until death do them part. At that moment, to confirm the couple's covenant, the officiant pronounces the marriage "in the name of the Father, and of the Son, and of the Holy Spirit." That is, in the name of the Triune God and in the presence of many witnesses, he affirms that the bride and groom have finally become one flesh. Because God's holy name is at stake, no one but God can break the covenant. "Therefore what God has joined together, let not man separate" (Matt. 19:6; Mark 10:9).

Nevertheless, imperfect human beings break their marriage covenant before God because of personality differences, or for one reason or another. Worldly people aside, Christian couples who believe in the Triune God should remember that divorce is a blasphemy against God's name. Didn't they make solemn vows in

God's name on their wedding day?

In the name of God, I, Ryul Kwon, take you, Mi Ae Son, to be my wife, to have and to hold from this day forward, for better, for worse, for richer, for poorer, in sickness and in health, to love and to cherish, until we are parted by death. This is my solemn vow.

Except in very rare cases (adultery, violence, etc.), you must honor your vows to God. Even in those cases, they should try to repair the relationship as best they can. When a Christian couple divorces, it is not just about them. Recall His Word (Eph. 5:31-32) that He wants to demonstrate the mystical union of Christ and the church through the relationship of husband and wife. Therefore, when a couple breaks the covenant, God perceives it as a break in the relationship between Christ and the church. We must clearly remember that for Christians, divorce is tantamount to the destruction of the body of Christ.

Next, when couples divorce, they leave their children with scars that cannot be washed away. As a party to this case, I can vividly testify. No matter how much a couple fights and argues behind their children's backs, their children are always watching. When I was a child, my parents fought in secret. One day, after putting two sons to bed deeply, my father one-sidedly assaulted and verbally abused my mother, and I happened to wake up and see it. I was so scared at such a young age, but I just pretended not to notice and continued to sleep. I can still vividly remember my father yelling at my grandmother with a kitchen knife that he would kill her for meddling in their marital affairs.

You will fight tooth and nail against your spouse because of your mismatched personalities, but keep in mind that your children who watch unknowingly will suffer terrible trauma! I hated my father tooth and nail, and even when I went to church, there was a latent hatred in my heart for him. But when he passed away, God gave me a forgiving heart, so I could not stop crying in front of his body. Now, more than 20 years later, I miss him sometimes. I wish he could see his grandchildren.

And the divorce of a couple has a huge impact on being parents of children. I vowed to myself that I would never be like my father, and I gritted my teeth and tried my best not to be a husband like him when I got married. By God's grace, my temperament was tempered, and fortunately, the tyrannical husband aspect of my father completely disappeared. However, problems began to appear when I raised my children. My behavior toward my children seemed to be familiar. One day, I scolded my second son harshly, and as I watched him get shocked, I saw myself freaking out over my father's verbal abuse decades earlier. I blamed myself so much and regretted that night. I realized the importance of my relationship with my father. I felt that I could only be as good a father to my own children as I had been to my own father.

Fortunately, that part of me is now gone. I would never want to pass on the trauma of that boy from decades ago to my three sons. Although I had an unhealthy relationship with my physical father, I now have an abundant loving relationship with my Heavenly Father. I want to pass on the great and wonderful love I have received from my Heavenly Father to my sons. I try to do better than I used to, but there are still many areas where I fall short as a father in the eyes of my wife and of my children. I will continue to strive not to be an embarrassing father.

🎁 The Bizarre World of Divorce Today

According to the latest *Marriage and Divorce Statistics* from 2023, there were 194,000 marriages and 92,000 divorces in Korea.[84] This includes divorces with foreigners and divorces by age, but if you do the math, the divorce rate in 2023 was over 47.4%. This means that almost one out of every two married couples will divorce for one reason or another.

Nowadays, there are a lot more reasons for divorce than in the

★
84) 김경미, "2023년 혼인 이혼 통계", 『통계청 누리집』, 2024년 3월 19일, https://www.kostat.go.kr/board.es?mid=a10301010000&bid=204&act=view&list_no=429995.

past. While previous generations were primarily concerned with domestic violence, verbal abuse, and habitual adultery, there are many other reasons for divorce that would make little sense to our parents' generation (60+). A recent survey of divorced singles found that the number one reason for divorce was a spouse's rise to the top.[85] What this mean is that when a person's self-esteem is boosted by their success at work, it creates a disconnect between the couple, which leads to conflict. Even as a man in my mid-40s, I don't understand this. I would think that a spouse would be happy to see their spouse rise in the workforce, but that doesn't seem to be the case with this generation.

There is even an "Excel divorce," which means that couples divide the time and money they spend on their marriage by organizing it in an Excel program, and then divorce if it doesn't work out.[86] For example, if a husband or a wife wants to buy something, the person who is going to use it has to pay for it. And if they want to buy something that will be used by both of them, they have to pay for it from a joint account. Even they have to or-

---

★

85) Remarriage information company ONLY-U and marriage information company BENARAE conducted a survey on the perceptions of 556 divorced single men and women who want to remarry nationwide on what they consider to be the strengths of their ex-spouses that contributed to their divorce. 조유경, "돌싱男女 이혼 원인 물어보니...성격·외도 아닌 바로 '이것'", 『동아일보』 2024년 5월 11일, https://www.donga.com/news/article/all/20240511/124891050/2.

86) 김혜영, "'예비신랑' 조세호, 반반결혼 트렌드에 고개 갸웃 "엑셀은 좀..."(유퀴즈)", 『iMBC연예』 2024년 9월 5일, https://enews.imbc.com/News/RetrieveNewsInfo/429040.

Chapter 8 Divorce, Remarriage, and Reality

231

ganize their household chores in Excel. If this doesn't work out in the marriage, they casually tell each other that they will use it as grounds for divorce.

And for an Excel divorce to be finalized, there must be an "Excel marriage." In fact, the latest trend in marriage among the MZ generation (especially those in their 20s and 30s) is called the "50/50 marriage." This is because it costs a lot of money to get married, so they split everything 50/50. The idea is that when you get married, you each contribute half to the wedding fund, and then you keep a separate account for living expenses and put money into it to run the household. This may seem very reasonable, but it's actually based on selfishness: "I only want to pay half, and I don't want to pay more.[87] This is a very unfamiliar view of marriage to the older generation, regardless of faith.

The problem is that there are young couples in the church who have this view of marriage. In fact, this was the case with one couple I counseled. Even though the husband is a pastor, the wife has an Excel spreadsheet of what each of them is supposed to do, and she keeps it on the wall. Out of consideration for her husband, she divided the household chores to the days when he doesn't go to church. Even so, I've heard her complain that her husband

---

87) 추영, "반반결혼, 엑셀이혼…요즘 부부들이 사는 법", 『웨딩TV』 2024년 2월 16일, https://www.wedd.tv/news/articleView.html?idxno=8533.

don't fulfill his obligations. As a couple who have been married for 20 years, my wife and I couldn't understand their problems.

Therefore, we need to approach the issue of divorce differently than previous generations. What was taken for granted in the past is now a serious reason for divorce for MZ couples. Even if they go to church and have faith, their view of marriage is definitely different from their parents' generation. If we start approaching it as a matter of right and wrong, the conversation may be cut off. The same may be true of *A Theology for Married Couples*. I think this book can be spiritually challenging and inspiring for older generations, but I wonder how it will be for MZ couples who have the same view of marriage as Excel marriage and 50/50 marriage. Nevertheless, I have a holy burden to share a view of marriage based on the Bible and the gospel.

A Biblical Ground for Divorce #1:
Adultery of a Spouse

While the Bible prohibits divorce in principle, it does allow it in very specific cases. According to Jesus' words, divorce is allowed when a spouse commits adultery. Let's look at Matthew 19:3-12 to see what Jesus meant. One day the Pharisees came to Jesus and asked Him this question. "Is it lawful for a man to divorce his wife for *just* any reason?" (v. 3). They weren't asking for serious advice on divorce, but rather to test Him. Jesus responded by referring them to a passage in Genesis.

> 4 And He answered and said to them, "Have you not read that He who made *them* at the beginning *'made them male and female,'* 5 and said, *'For this reason a man shall leave his father and mother and be joined to his wife, and the two shall become one flesh'*? 6 So then, they are no longer two but one flesh. Therefore what God has joined together, let not man separate." (Matt. 19:4-6)

As you can see, in verses 4-5, Jesus refers to Genesis 1:27[88] and 2:24[89] and draws His conclusion in verse 6, which is that since husband and wife are no longer two, but one flesh, as God established the institution of marriage in the beginning, no man can separate what God has joined together.

But the Pharisees don't back down and continue their questioning. "Why then did Moses command to give a certificate of divorce, and to put her away?" (v. 7). Here their understanding of the Mosaic Law becomes clear: they thought that God's original

★

88) So God created man in His *own* image; in the image of God He created him; male and female He created them.

89) Therefore a man shall leave his father and mother and be joined to his wife, and they shall become one flesh.

purpose for marriage had been "effectively replaced by Moses' regulations."[90] That is, a man could get married and then give his wife a divorce certificate and put her away. But what Jesus is saying is that the Mosaic Law does not replace God's original intent, but merely reflects the reality of imperfect human beings (v. 8).

This is actually an important principle when we read the Bible. We tend to read statements in the Old Testament as if they were God's original intentions. For example, when we read accounts of warfare in the Old Testament, some church members argue that we should use force, as Israel did in the Old Testament, to deal with groups we consider evil. War was not God's original intention, but rather a temporary means for God to use Israel to demonstrate His power to the world by showing us how imperfect human beings live after sin. In the New Testament, Jesus spoke of God's original intent when He said, "Put your sword in its place, for all who take the sword will perish by the sword" (Matt. 26:52).

Similarly, the divorce regulation[91] in the Mosaic Law was not the original purpose of God. Divorce should never have happened, but it should be understood as a reflection of the corrupt mar-

★

90) 안드레아스 쾨스텐버거 외, 『성경의 눈으로 본 결혼과 가정(보급판)』, 윤종석 옮김 (서울: 아바서원, 2024), 291.

91) "When a man takes a wife and marries her, and it happens that she finds no favor in his eyes because he has found some uncleanness in her, and he writes her a certificate of divorce, puts *it* in her hand, and sends her out of his house, (Deut. 24:1).

riage culture of the time and as a minimum measure to discourage imprudent divorce in those circumstances. Their question, "Why then did Moses command to give a certificate of divorce, and to put her away?" reveals their usual hidden intent: If you are married and don't like your wife, it is perfectly acceptable to write her a certificate of divorce and put her away, based on an arbitrary interpretation of "some uncleanness in her" (Deut. 24:1).

Then Jesus said, "And I say to you, whoever divorces his wife, except for sexual immorality, and marries another, commits adultery" (v. 9). In other words, to those who thought they could just give her a certificate of divorce and put her away if they found something unfaithful in her, Jesus said that there should never be any reason to abandon a wife "except for sexual immorality." Interestingly, even the disciples are surprised by Jesus' words. "If such is the case of the man with *his* wife, it is better not to marry" (v. 10). It seems that the disciples, like the Jews of that time, thought Jesus' words were too strict.

However, if we look at Jesus' words more closely, we see that while He strictly regulated divorce, He also wanted us to be able to forgive our immoral spouses. In fact, Jesus offered forgiveness and love to a woman caught in the act of adultery (John 7:53-8:11). In summary, while first-century Jews "arbitrarily" (though not always) interpreted the divorce laws to make divorce mandatory, Jesus seems to have permitted it only when a spouse commits adultery.[92] That is to say, while divorce is truly necessary because of a spouse's infidelity, it is sometimes possible to forgive and restore the relationship.

How can we apply Jesus' words to married couples today? First, we must remember that no one can separate the marriage relationship that God has joined together for the purpose of marriage. I think many Christian couples often forget that they have been "joined together by God." The fact that you meet and spend your life with one person out of all the people in the world is something that could not have happened without God's providence. You chose him/her, but you must remember God's hand behind the scenes to make that choice. If you are currently considering divorce, I encourage you to meditate on God's providence in your life.

Second, don't make up your own grounds for divorce. We should learn from the Pharisees of Jesus' day, who used arbitrary interpretations of the divorce regulation in the law to justify putting away their wives. Today, husbands and wives are making up all sorts of reasons for divorce without any real need. Consider the Excel divorce phenomenon I mentioned earlier. It's a list of things that people make up as they see fit, and if they don't meet them, they blame their spouse and try to get an easy divorce. Instead of

★
92) 안드레아스 쾨스텐버거 외, 『성경의 눈으로 본 결혼과 가정(보급판)』 292.

seeing the covenant of marriage as a solemn promise to be honored for the rest of their lives, they see it as an event in their lives, especially if they don't have children yet. They think they can move on and start over with someone else.

The world aside, we Christians are to follow the words of Jesus. If you think that you and your spouse are so incompatible that you can't live together, consider the heart of our Bridegroom, Jesus. Do you think Jesus is so compatible with His bride (us) that He will stay with her forever? During the pandemic, I was doing a virtual book concert and someone asked me how I felt about divorce. Naturally, I replied that according to the Bible, a spouse should never divorce "except for sexual immorality." Later, I was told that she was outraged by my answer and protested that I did not know how hard it is to live with an incompatible spouse. I know how hard it is. For a while, my wife would have said to me, "Our marriage is like the lottery." But now we're considerate of each other and we love each other more than ever.

Third, even if your spouse has committed adultery, you should forgive him/her and try again to restore the relationship. Of course, I realize that this is not easy to say. It may be easy for the cheating spouse to say forgive and restore the relationship, but it may be very difficult for the other spouse who is suffering. Furthermore, it takes a long time to forgive and restore a relationship. Especially for a wife who has suffered through her husband's infidelity, the trauma is long lasting, and every time you're in the bedroom with him, you're reminded of what he did, and it's really hard to let go. Of course, the opposite is not much different.

However, if the person is sincerely remorseful and repentant, it may be worthwhile to work toward forgiveness and restoration. The offending spouse should make a vow to God never to have an affair again and prove over time that the vow is sincere. You should also take the time to listen to and unconditionally understand all of your hurt partner's reactions. You have no words to defend yourself. So you must sincerely accept the painful feelings your spouse is expressing and live your life with an apologetic heart until the words "Now it's okay!" come out of his/her mouth. And you should spend more time than ever making new memories together. You should frequently make happy times for your spouse and for yourself, as if you were rekindling your premarital relationship. Then, by God's grace, you will experience a more mature love than before.

A Biblical Ground for Divorce #2: Refusal of an Unbelieving Spouse

The second biblical ground for divorce is the refusal of a non-Christian spouse to remain in the marriage. Paul gave the Corinthian church this instruction: "But if the unbeliever departs, let him depart; a brother or a sister is not under bondage in such *cases*" (1 Cor. 7:15). You might be surprised to learn that this is not a teaching of Jesus. However, since Jesus ministered primarily among the Jews, He did not leave any teaching on the so-called "mixed marriages" that were occurring in the mission field of the Hellenic region where Paul worked.[93]

In the first century, Corinth was a port city with a high level of immorality and idolatry. As Paul's evangelistic mission established churches and brought believers to them, mixed marriages became a problem. There were many cases where only one spouse believed in Jesus and the other was an unbeliever. In this situation, Paul gives practical instructions to the believers. If the unbelieving spouse asks for a separation, they can simply divorce.

However, we should approach Paul's statement with caution. In our context today, when an unbelieving spouse asks for separation, it feels very different from simply divorcing than it did in Paul's day. Today, it's rare for an unbeliever to blatantly force his/her spouse into idolatry or to persecute him/her for his/her faith. But that was the atmosphere in Corinth in the first century. When the Corinthians were being asked to believe in a Man named Jesus, whom they had never heard of or seen, as God, it was very

★
93) 김세윤, 『고린도전서 강해(개정판)』 (서울: 두란노, 2008), 133.

difficult for those who actually believed to maintain their marriages as they had before. How could Christians, who had been taught to "flee sexual immorality" (1 Cor. 6:18), go back to the temple and engage in idolatry combined with sexual activity?

If an unbelieving spouse who insists on such routines says he/she can no longer stay in the marriage, then simply separate. (Unlike Jewish society, Greek custom in Corinth allowed a woman to file for divorce.) Paul affirms that a brother or sister in Jesus need not be bound by these things. Why is this? Because as holy Christians united to Christ, they can no longer participate in idolatry. Nevertheless, Paul counsels not to abandon an unbelieving spouse if he/she like living with him/her (7:12-13). Of course, this assumes that the spouse is not forcing the partner to worship idols or persecuting his/her faith. Paul's reasoning is that the unbelieving spouse might be sanctified through the believing husband or wife (7:14). It's a missional mindset that a person who is currently in a mixed marriage could be sanctified by a believing spouse.

Paul's teaching has very practical applications for us today. In fact, it can be taken literally. In the Korean church, there are quite a few couples where only one believes in Jesus. In such cases, if the unbelieving spouse likes to live with his/her partner, he/she should follow Paul's advice and live together instead of divorcing. This is because the husband or wife may come to believe in Jesus through the believing spouse. Over the course of a lifetime, he/she will be unintentionally influenced by the gospel through the life of the believing spouse. Of course, there are many cases in which the unbelieving spouse influences the partner more and causes him/her to backslide. Nevertheless, a believing husband or wife should trust God and pray for the power of the gospel to reach their spouse.

However, if an unbelieving spouse openly persecutes the partner's faith and refuses to stay in the marriage, the partner can follow Paul's counsel and divorce without restraint. Of course, in this case, the partner should try again to live with the spouse in the hope that he/she will change, but if he/she shows no signs of change, divorce should be considered as a last resort. However, if the partner decides to persevere for the sake of the children, he/she should be prepared for persecution and find a way to live out the faith as wisely as possible.

Unstated Grounds for Divorce

Now we're going to take a more realistic approach. We're going to deal with cases that are not explicitly mentioned in the Bible, but could be grounds for divorce. We shouldn't be overly literal in our understanding of the Bible's statements. So it would be a stretch to argue that the only grounds for divorce mentioned in the Bible are adultery and the refusal of an unbelieving spouse to stay in the marriage. This is because the circumstances of those who lived in biblical times are so different from those we face today.

This is already evidenced in the case of Paul, who, although a contemporary of the first century, had to answer the question of mixed marriages as he preached the gospel in a completely different context from that of Jesus' ministry. He was clearly aware of Jesus' teachings through the other apostles, but he was now building on them and applying them anew with a theological response that was consistent with God's will in the new context. That is, he did not take a literal, legalistic understanding of Jesus' teaching about spousal adultery as a ground for divorce and insist that it was the only one that could be applied in the new context. To put it another way, he did not tell the Corinthian church who were living with unbelieving spouses that they should never divorce their spouses except in the case of adultery. He did so in full consideration of the religious persecution that an idolatrous spouse might inflict on a believing husband or wife.

Similarly, in the context in which we live today, there are many situations in which we may encounter situations that Paul does not mention. For example, consider the case of a Christian wife who is repeatedly beaten by her husband. It's not like he's cheating on her or refusing to stay married. In this case alone, it doesn't qualify as either of the two biblical grounds for divorce. What's more, the husband's domestic violence shows no signs of subsiding, and the wife is putting up with it for the sake of her children. The wife goes to the pastor of her church and asks for counseling, but the pastor advises her to pray and persevere because it is not a biblical ground for divorce. So the wife tries again, praying and persevering, but her husband's assaults and verbal abuse become worse and worse, until she is unable to carry on with her daily life.

If this is the case, she should be isolated from her husband with the help of others. And while the church cannot recommend divorce, if the victim wife wishes to divorce, she should be allowed to do so. Do you think God would say that such a wife should continue to suffer at the hands of her husband and remain married? Of course not. In fact, we can interpret this as Paul's grounds for divorce. If an unbelieving spouse refuses to stay in the marriage, Paul recommends that the partner should depart, not tied down. A husband who repeatedly assaults his wife and still claims to be a Christian should be considered an unbeliever in the gospel. And even if he does not reject the marriage first, we should interpret such a horrible situation as a rejection of a normal marriage. This interpretation is perhaps in line with Paul's attempts to make new interpretations and answers based on the teachings of Jesus in each new situation he encountered.

There are many other grounds for divorce for a Christian couple besides a husband's repeated assault. One thing that is clear is that while God truly values the marriage covenant of Christians, He does not want either party to be left in excruciating pain as a result of trying to honor that covenant. He would never want a spouse and children to continue to live in such an environment. Of course, it would be wonderful if, after praying and enduring, the person is dramatically changed and becomes a new person. But if you don't think that's likely, you should respect the sufferer's decision.

We also recognize that creating grounds for divorce in this way runs the risk of encouraging Christians to divorce themselves. Therefore, divorce matters should not be left to the judgment of the parties alone, but should be carefully guided by the church and follow the official legal process.[94] At the church level, we must evaluate and determine whether the couple's situation truly warrants divorce, modeling Paul's theological thinking. The couple should be counseled that divorce is a last resort for Christians, and they should be counseled to seek God's guidance carefully.

The Cases in Which You Can Remarry

In the previous section, we looked at the cases where divorce

---

★

94) See the Westminster Confession of Faith, Ch 24.6.

is permitted in the Bible. It's important to note that we cannot always say that when divorce is permitted, remarriage is permitted. Rather, the Bible encourages divorced people to stay alone as much as possible and even to reconcile. Of course, enough time should have passed for them to fully forgive each other and to be able to love again.

> 10 Now to the married I command, *yet* not I but the Lord: A wife is not to depart from *her* husband. 11 But even if she does depart, let her remain unmarried or be reconciled to *her* husband. And a husband is not to divorce *his* wife. (1 Cor. 7:10-11)

This is Paul's exhortation to the Corinthian church. He allows divorce when necessary, but strictly forbids remarriage. He reminds them that it is the Lord, not himself, who commands it. If they do divorce, he encourages them to stay alone or to reconcile with their spouse. This is likely because the Corinthians were an immoral people, and if their faith weakened after divorce, they would probably be in danger of repeating of remarrying someone else.

Jesus also strictly regulated remarriage. "Whoever divorces his wife and marries another commits adultery against her. And if a woman divorces her husband and marries another, she commits adultery" (Mark 10:11-12). Of course, in the parallel text, Matthew 19, Jesus makes an exception. "And I say to you, whoever divorces his wife, except for sexual immorality, and marries another, commits adultery; and whoever marries her who is divorced commits adultery" (v. 9). That is, Jesus made it a condition for remarriage that the spouse commit sexual immorality.

Then there's another case: we can remarry someone else if the spouse dies.

> 2 For the woman who has a husband is bound by the law to *her* husband as long as he lives. But if the husband dies, she is released from the law of *her* husband. 3 So then if, while *her* husband lives, she marries another man, she will be called an adulteress; but if her husband dies, she is free from that law, so that she is no adulteress, though she has married another man. (Rom. 7:2-3)

This passage says that if you divorce and remarry someone else, it is adultery because your marriage is still valid as long as your spouse is alive, but if you remarry after your spouse dies, it is not adultery. That is, the death of a spouse is a condition for remarriage to another person. On your wedding day, you made a solemn vow before God to love and serve each other "until death do us part." Therefore, as long as your spouse is alive, it is not permissible to divorce and remarry someone else.

To summarize, there are two conditions under which a person can remarry. There are two conditions: if your spouse commits sexual immorality[95] and if your spouse dies. In the former case, there is some possibility of being reunited with your spouse, but in the latter case, it is force majeure (i.e., an act of God) and a complete separation. The overall context of the Bible, as discussed earlier, is that even if a spouse has committed sexual immorality, every effort should be made to restore the relationship by bringing him/her to genuine repentance. In this context, the most obvious condition for remarriage is the death of the spouse.

Why does the Bible state this principle? As I see it, it boils down to two things. First, because God set up one man and one woman to be married[96] and as long as the couple is alive, this marriage covenant has special significance. The marriage covenant, vowed and made before God, is the most solid shadow of an eternal substance (the relationship between Christ and the church), and it continues in effect as long as both parties are alive. It is similar to how Christ, the Bridegroom, never abandons His bride, the church. So it seems that even in the case of divorce, the previous marriage covenant remains valid before God as long as both spouses (the former husband and wife) are alive. (This

★

95) Strictly speaking, it's a broader term that includes adultery, but I've used it to mean "adultery" in practice.

96) In the marriage verse, Genesis 2:24, both "a man" and "his wife" are singular.

may be why Paul exhorted those who had been separated to remain separated or to be united again.) If a divorced spouse meets someone else and remarries, they are entering into another marriage covenant, which is contrary to God's will that marriage be between one man and one woman. In God's eyes, it is as if the divorced spouse is entering into two marriage covenants at the same time. (Assuming God does not accept their divorce.) Therefore, the death of a spouse is the only sure condition for remarriage.

Second, because the marriage covenant ceases to function after the death of one spouse. This is actually a restatement of the first reason. Since Christian marriage is a shadow of the eternal substance, once the deceased spouse has gone to be with the eternal Bridegroom, neither spouse alone can any longer reveal the mystical union of Christ and the church. Therefore, when one spouse dies, the marriage covenant ceases to function and the couple is free from its law and can remarry.

In the larger discourse of the resurrection, there is an inevitable reason why the marriage covenant between a husband and wife should end at death. At the time of the resurrection, when the kingdom of God is consummated, there will be no more marriage and no more giving in marriage (Matt. 22:30). In other words, the institution of marriage will no longer exist, because the substance of the perfect and eternal marriage (the mystical union of Christ and the church) has arrived. At that time, all Christians will have

God as their Father and will exist only as literal brothers and sisters. All earthly ties, including those of husband and wife, will cease to exist, and they will exist only as the bride of Christ, the eternal Bridegroom. Therefore, the marriage covenant between husband and wife on this earth must be a temporary shadow, and its function must end after death, so that the appearance of the resurrection spoken of by the Lord can be fulfilled. Otherwise, if the marriage covenant were to continue after death, there would be great confusion in family relationships (especially among remarried couples) at the resurrection.

🎁 Realistic Problems of Remarriage

The reality is that there are couples who remarry for reasons that are not biblically grounds for remarriage. There are many such couples in the church, as well as in the world. That is to say, it is not uncommon for a former husband or wife to divorce and remarry for other reasons, even if they have not committed adultery or died. For example, a wife may divorce her husband because he is a habitual abuser, gambler, or drug user and move on with her life. There are even cases where people divorce and remarry over something as "insignificant" as an Excel divorce or personality differences. How should we understand such people in these cases?

Technically, they have violated the biblical principle of remarriage (which is not meant to be condemnatory), but that doesn't mean they should abandon their remarried spouse and live alone again. It is even more impractical to divorce again and reunite with the person you were previously married to. Rather, the Bible says, "that *is* an abomination before the LORD" (Deut. 24:4).

The truth is, it's not easy to make judgments and give advice. Even among scholars who specialize in this area, there is no consensus. Nevertheless, I'd like to offer what I believe to be the most sound view, based on the Bible and taking into account practical issues. First of all, if we look for an example of such a case in the Bible, we find the Samaritan woman in John 4. When she came to draw water, Jesus asked her to "Give Me a drink" (v. 7). Normally, Jews don't associate with Samaritans, so she was puzzled that Jesus, a Jew, would make such a request of her. After Jesus teaches her what true living water is and says, "Go, call your husband, and come here" (v. 16), their conversation goes something like this.

17 The woman answered and said, "I have no husband." Jesus said to her, "You have well said, 'I have no husband,' 18 for you have had five husbands, and the one whom you now have is not your husband; in that you spoke truly." (John 4:17-18)

For some reason, the woman has a complicated past and has had five husbands. Even the man she's living with now doesn't seem to be her legal husband. In any case, given Jesus' wording "you have had five husbands," it seems likely that He recognized these men as her husbands, even though she had already remarried several times. Of course, this doesn't mean it's not a sin. We don't know what happened to the Samaritan woman, but she sinned by divorcing and remarrying many times, even though it was against the law. (In fact, her ex-husbands who abandoned her were the bigger sinners.) Yet Jesus doesn't condemn her for her history of divorce and previous remarriages, but recognizes her as she is. He did, of course, say that the current man living with her outside of the legal process was not her husband.

In any case, the case of the Samaritan woman shows us what attitude we should have toward remarried couples who exist in the reality of the church. Just as Jesus recognized her past remarriages in violation of the law, so we should recognize the remarriage of couples who are in violation of biblical teaching. Given that Jesus did not condemn the Samaritan woman, we have no right to condemn such remarried couples. Although they have remarried in an unbiblical decision, they have solemnly vowed again before God to establish a marriage covenant between them. With caution, I would say at this point that God breaks the previous marriage covenant of the divorced spouse and recognizes and renews the covenant of the remarried couple. This is because only God, who made the marriage covenant, has the right to break it.[97]

Of course, given the continuity of the covenant once made, it seems impossible for a couple to make another marriage covenant while their former spouse is still alive, as we have argued. But even so, God's grace in Christ to forgive them and sanctify them again is applied to them, so that God recognizes the marriage covenant they made before Him. God has given special significance to the marriage covenant, but He does not equate it with the spiritual marriage covenant between Christ the Bridegroom and the Church the Bride, because our marriage covenant is only a shadow of the eternal substance. Therefore, it is not reasonable to go to the extreme of claiming that because a marriage covenant, once made, is valid for life as long as the divorced spouse is alive, it is always illegal to remarry another.

Remarriage Is Not Always a Good Thing

It would be nice for a divorced person to find someone new and remarry, but that's not always the case. As I mentioned earlier, I grew up in a divorced family. My mother ran away from home

★

97) John Piper, *This Momentary Marriage*, 168.

when I was in elementary school, and because she couldn't live on her own, she met another man and started a new life. However, she met someone who was almost identical to her ex-husband, and she went through another difficult life. Her second husband was a drunk and abusive man, and she struggled with him until she died. Sometimes they seemed to have a good relationship, but in the eyes of her adult son, she just settled for a man who was a little off. Fortunately, my mother later came to faith in Jesus and closed her eyes with the hope of heaven.

The apostle Paul encourages divorced believers to remain as they are (1 Cor. 7:26). He even says that remarrying is good, but remaining the same is better and happier (7:40). Of course, Paul says such a thing "because of the present distress" (7:26). "The present distress" in his mind refers to the Roman Empire's imminent persecution of Christians, which, given the circumstances of the first century, is likely to happen sooner or later.[98] If he believes this to be the case, he suggests that divorced Christians would be well advised to focus their efforts on the kingdom of God and the gospel rather than on trying to please their spouses by remarrying.

We can apply Paul's theological thinking to us as well. Today,

★
98) 그랜트 오스본 편, 『LAB 주석 시리즈: 고린도전서』 김일우 옮김 (서울: 한국성서유니온선교회, 2002), 177.

with the exception of certain nations, we may not have the present distress that Paul speaks of. But as the Lord's return draws nearer, we can focus our energies on the kingdom of God and the gospel rather than on remarriage, believing that the tribulation of the world may be imminent sooner rather than later. It is good to remarry and enjoy the happiness of a new spouse, but it is even better to never remarry and devote the rest of your life to renewing the world, relying only on the Lord as your eternal Bridegroom.

It is up to the divorced Christians themselves to prayerfully decide what to do. It is not advisable to remarry because of the pressures and expectations of others. At the risk of sounding a bit frivolous, it is good to seriously consider the purpose for which God has called you as a divorced single. Of course, it's also perfectly fine to prayerfully consider remarrying so that you and your new spouse can become more committed to the kingdom of God and the gospel. It's up to you to discern what's best for you, led by the Holy Spirit.

🎁 One Day We Will Be Alone

No matter how happy we are in our marriage, we all end up alone at some point. It's just in a different order, but at some point we have to let go of our spouse and live our lives alone. In this sense, whether we are married, divorced, or remarried, we all must eventually be alone, trusting only in the Lord as our eternal Bridegroom.

Some Christians never marry and live their lives alone from the beginning. Others, like the apostle Paul, are single when they could have been married, but have a special mission for the kingdom of God and the church. They are to be commended. In the words of Jesus, they "have made themselves eunuchs for the kingdom of heaven's sake" (Matt. 19:12), which means that they are fully committed to the kingdom of God, abstaining from sexual desires, whether male or female. However, "intentional singles" who live alone because they don't want to be tied down are not very desirable in the eyes of the Lord.

We should indeed value the Christian marriage, but we should not fall into *marriageism*, that is, criticizing unmarried (or unsuccessful) Christians as if there is something wrong with them and judging their faith based on their marital status. I have acquaintances who have been single their entire lives and remain steadfastly committed to the kingdom of God and the gospel. Even though they are well past the age of sixty, they still trust the Lord with all their hearts and spend their lives longing for the eternal kingdom. Although they do not have a physical spouse, they love the Lord, the perfect Bridegroom, and bear witness in another way to the mystical union of Christ and the church. Perhaps they do so in a more direct way than those of us who are married.

We must remember that one day we will be alone. That's why you should love and serve your spouse even more than you do now. We should cherish and love each other until death do us part, with the idea that you are precious because you are not forever. And when your spouse is called home by God, you should literally spend the rest of your life happily with God alone. Rather than remarrying, it would be better to spend the rest of our lives fully devoted to the kingdom of God and the gospel, eagerly waiting for the Lord's return. And then, when God calls us home, we will finally meet our spouse in Paradise.

1. Have you ever wanted to divorce your spouse because of him/her? Answer this question inwardly, of course, and think about why.

2. Why do you think phenomena like Excel divorces happen? And what would you say to a couple you know who are about to divorce for that reason?

3. If you had church members who were suffering because of an unbelieving spouse, how would you comfort and counsel them?

4. Have you ever thought about the fact that one day you will be alone? And before that moment arrives, what kind of mindset and attitude do you want to have for the rest of your life with your spouse?

EPILOGUE

Dreaming of the Perfect Day

We have come to the end of *A Theology for Married Couples*. As I said in *A Theology of Dating*, "theology" (*theologia*, in Latin) means that "God says to us" or "We say about God."[99] So *A Theology for Married Couples* means that a husband and wife who believe in Jesus say about God in their daily lives and listen to what God is saying to them. Christian couples are distinct from those of the world. They live as happily as possible in this world, and when death separates them, there is no more hope. In fact, death is the saddest and most dreaded thing for couples of the world.

But for us, the death they dread is only a step in the process of meeting our eternal and perfect Bridegroom. On that day, we will

★
99) 유해무, 『개혁교의학』 (고양: 크리스챤다이제스트, 1997), 21.

witness the substance of the marriage covenant as experienced on earth. We will realize that the vow to love each other and to remain faithful to one another in all things, in joy and in sorrow, in health and in sickness, in wealth and in poverty, is now directed to the eternal Bridegroom. There will be no more sorrow, no more pain, no more death, but only the fullness of happiness, where the perfect Bridegroom loves us all, His holy Bride, supremely.

But it is not over yet. In Paradise, where our souls will dwell after death, we will await our final resurrection with the perfect Bridegroom. We will rejoice with him/her with whom we once shared our lives, and we will watch in anticipation as the beautiful Eden that God created in the beginning is restored and perfected on earth. At the Lord's return, we will all be transformed into glorified resurrection bodies and live in endless bliss with Him forever as His perfect and holy Bride in the all-new kingdom of God.

To all the husbands and wives of the world, aren't you looking forward to this day? Don't you want to dedicate your life together as a couple to the work that will bring it about? May you deeply realize the noble purpose for which God has called you and your spouse to love each other as a couple with a mission for His kingdom.

 BIBLIOGRAPHY

▓ BIBLES

Biblia Hebraica Stuttgartensia. With Werkgroep Informatica, Vrije Universiteit Morphology; Bible. O.T. Hebrew. Werkgroep Informatica, Vrije Universiteit. Logos Bible Software, 2006.

Novum Testamentum Graece. Edited by Barbara Aland, Kurt Aland, Johannes Karvidopoulos, Carlo M. Martini, and Bruce M. Metzger, 28th ed. Stuttgart: Deutsche Bibelgesellschaft, 2012.

The Holy Bible. English Standard Version. Wheaton: Crossway Bibles, 2016.

The Holy Bible. New American Standard Bible. La Habra, CA: The Lockman Foundation, 1995.

The Holy Bible. New International Version. Grand Rapids, MI: Zondervan, 2011.

The Holy Bible. New King James Version. Nashville: Thomas Nelson, 1982.

The New Testament in the Original Greek: Byzantine Textform. Edited by Maurice A. Robinson and William G. Pierpont. Southborough, MA: Chilton Book Publishing, 2005.

▓ ENGLISH BOOKS

Bauer, Walter. *A Greek-English Lexicon of the New Testament and Other Early Christian Literature*. Revised and edited by Frederick William Danker, 3rd. ed. Chicago: The University of Chicago Press, 2000.

Hamilton. Victor P. *The Book of Genesis, Chapters 1-17*. NICOT. Grand Rapids, MI: William B. Eerdmans Publishing Company, 1990.

Kwon, Ryul J. *A Theology of Dating: The Partial Shadow of Marriage*. Seoul: Overflowing Joy, 2022.

Lewis, C. S. *The Four Loves*. New York: Harcourt, Brace and Company, 1960.

Matthews, Victor Harold, Mark W. Chavalas, and John H. Walton. *The IVP Bible Background Commentary: Old Testament*. Electronic ed. Downers Grove, IL: InterVarsity Press, 2000.

Ortlund, Ray. *Marriage and the Mystery of the Gospel*. ed. Dane C. Ortlund and Miles Van Pelt. Short Studies in Biblical Theology. Wheaton, IL: Crossway, 2016.

Osborne, Grant R. *Revelation*. BECNT. Grand Rapids, MI: Baker Academic, 2002.

Piper, John. *This Momentary Marriage: A Parable of Permanence*. Wheaton, Illinois: Crossway Books, 2009.

Wichern, Sr., F. B. "Family Systems Therapy," in *Baker Encyclopedia of Psychology & Counseling*. Edited by David G. Benner and Peter C. Hill. Baker reference library. Grand Rapids, MI: Baker Books, 1999.

▓ KOREAN BOOKS

강병도 편. 『카리스 종합주석 제51권: 전도서, 아가』. 서울: 기독지혜사, 2014.

권기현. 『예배 중에 찾아오시는 우리 하나님』. 경산: 도서출판 R&F, 2019.

권율. 『간증의 재발견 시리즈 5. 전능자의 손길』. 서울: 세움북스, 2024.

길성남. 『에베소서 어떻게 읽을 것인가』. 서울: 한국성서유니온, 2005.

김세윤. 『고린도전서 강해(개정판)』. 서울: 두란노, 2008.

_____. 『하나님이 만드신 여성』. 서울: 두란노, 2004.

김주환. 『회복탄력성』. 고양: 위즈덤하우스, 2011.

배정훈, 우병훈, 조윤호. 『교부신학프로젝트 02. 초대 교회와 마음의 치료』. 군포: 다함, 2022.

송병현. 『엑스포지멘터리 창세기』. 서울: 국제제자훈련원, 2010.

송웅달. 『900일간의 폭풍 사랑』. 서울: 김영사, 2007.

신국원. 『신국원의 문화 이야기』. 서울: 한국기독학생회출판부, 2002.

양용의. 『마태복음 어떻게 읽을 것인가(개정판)』. 서울: 한국성서유니온선교회, 2018.

유해무. 『개혁교의학』. 고양: 크리스챤다이제스트, 1997.

정민교. 『간증의 재발견 시리즈 3. 빛 가운데로 걸어가면』. 서울: 세움북스, 2023.

한정건. 『대한예수교장로회고신총회 설립 60주년 기념: 성경주석 창세기』. 서울: 고신총회출판국, 2016.

황영철. 『이 비밀이 크도다』. 의정부: 드림북, 2017.

황지영. 『사이좋은 부모생활』. 서울: 아르카, 2022.

김학모 편역. 『개혁주의 신앙고백』. 서울: 부흥과개혁사, 2015.

라헤이, 팀, 비벌리 라헤이. 『결혼행전』. 김인화 옮김. 서울: 생명의말씀사, 2005.

바우마이스터, 로이 F. 『소모되는 남자』. 서은국, 신지은, 이화령 옮김. 서울: 시그마북스, 2015.

에드워즈, 조나단. 『아메리카 P&R 시리즈 2. 신앙과 정서(개정역판)』. 서문강 옮김. 서울: 지평서원, 2009.

오스본, 그랜트 편. 『LAB 주석 시리즈: 고린도전서』. 김일우 옮김. 서울: 한국성서유니온선교회, 2002.

월트키, 브루스. 『NICOT 잠언 I』. 황의무 옮김. 서울: 부흥과개혁사, 2020.

채프먼, 게리. 『5가지 사랑의 언어』. 장동숙, 황을호 옮김. 서울: 생명의말씀사, 2010.

켈러, 팀. 『팀 켈러, 결혼을 말하다』. 최종훈 옮김. 서울: 두란노, 2014.

쾨스텐버거, 안드레아스, 데이비드 존스. 『성경의 눈으로 본 결혼과 가정(보급판)』. 윤종석 옮김. 서울: 아바서원, 2024.

프레임, 존. 『존 프레임의 조직신학』. 김진운 옮김. 서울: 부흥과개혁사, 2017.

휘트, 에드, 게이 휘트. 『즐거움을 위한 성』. 권영석, 송경숙 옮김. 서울: 한국기독학생회출판부, 2000.

■ WEBSITES

BrainyQuote. "A. P. Herbert Quotes." Accessed December 17, 2024. https://www.brainyquote.com/quotes/a_p_herbert_106679.

Merriam-Webster. "boredom." Accessed January 10, 2025. https://www.merriam-webster.com/dictionary/boredom.

A Theology for Married Couples

Oscar Wilde online. "A Woman of No Importance." Accessed December 17, 2024. https://www.wilde-
online.info/a-woman-of-no-importance-page12.html.

김경미. "2023년 혼인 이혼 통계". 『통계청 누리집』. 2024년 3월 19일. https://www.kostat.go.kr/board.es?mid
=a10301010000&bid=204&act=view&list_no =429995.

김혜영. "'예비신랑' 조세호, 반반결혼 트렌드에 고개 갸웃 "엑셀은 좀…"(유퀴즈)". 『iMBC연예』. 2024년 9월 5일.
https://enews.imbc.com/News/RetrieveNews Info/429040.

송민원. "하나님의 여성성을 나타내는 "라함(ᴘᴎᴄ)"에 대한 묵상". Institute for Biblical Preaching. 2021년 8월
25일. https://ibp.or.kr/wordspostachio/?bmode =view&idx=7632817.

오상훈. ""배우자가 이유 없이 짜증난다"… 부부 10명 중 6명 겪는 '권태기' 극복 비결 물어보니". 『헬스조선』.
2024년 4월 17일. https://health.chosun.com/site/data/html_dir/2024/04/16/2024041602351.html.

유경상. "이혼 변호사 최유나 "살인자 피고 무서워, 치약·분리수거 탓 이혼 많아"". 『뉴스엔미디어』. 2022년 10월
26일. https://www.newsen.com/news_view.php?uid=202210260532061710#google_vignette.

조유경. "돌싱男女 이혼 원인 물어보니…성격·외도 아닌 바로 '이것'". 『동아일보』. 2024년 5월 11일. https://
www.donga.com/news/article/all/20240511/12489105 0/2.

추영. "반반결혼, 엑셀이혼…요즘 부부들이 사는 법". 『웨딩TV』. 2024년 2월 16일. https://www.wedd.tv/news/
articleView.html?idxno=8533.